Paintings, Drawings
&
Photography

by

Shannon Schober
Vol.1

Paintings, Drawings & Photography
By Shannon Schober Vol. 1

Vitality

1240 Brevard Rd
Suite 1
Asheville NC
28806

ISBN 978-0-9818677-1-7

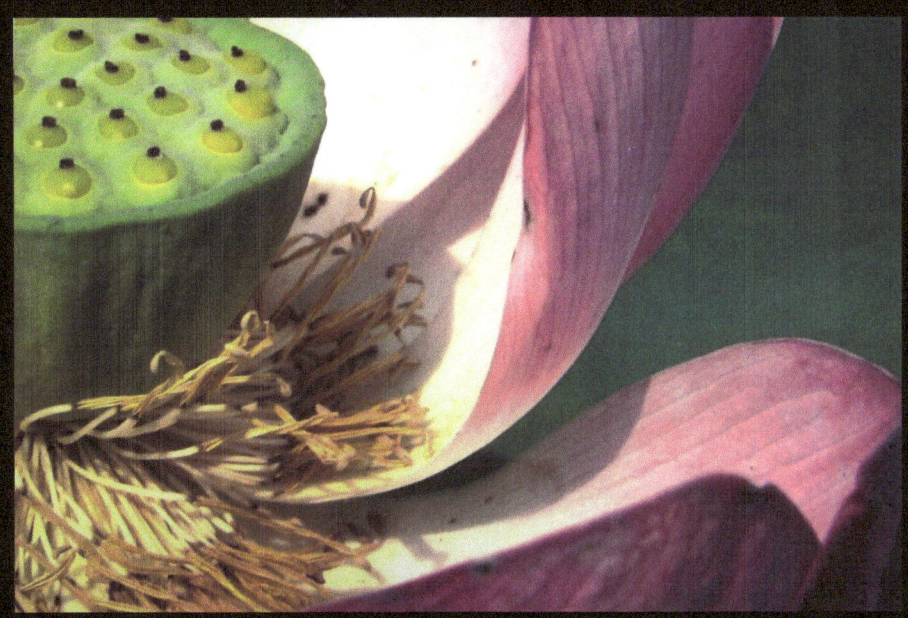

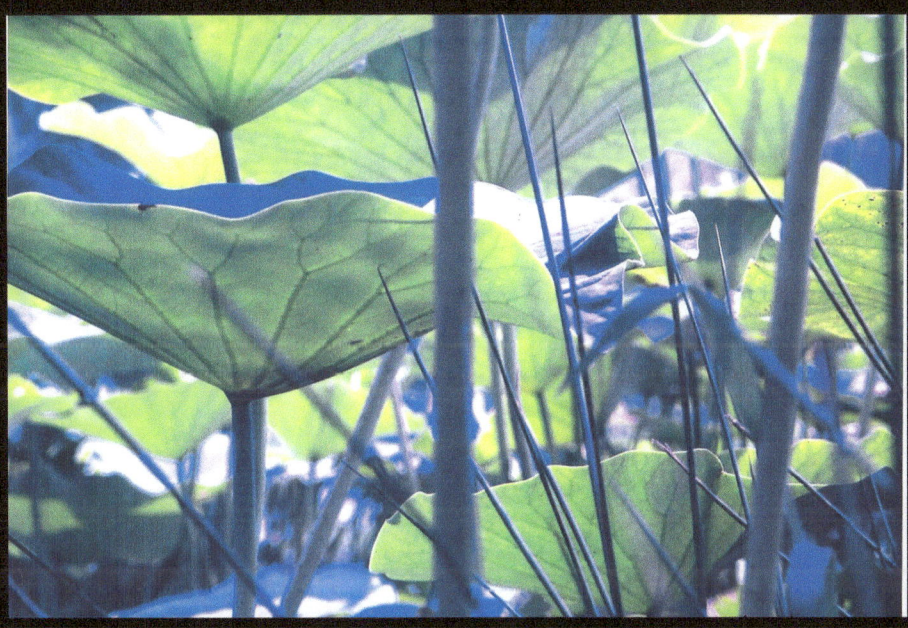

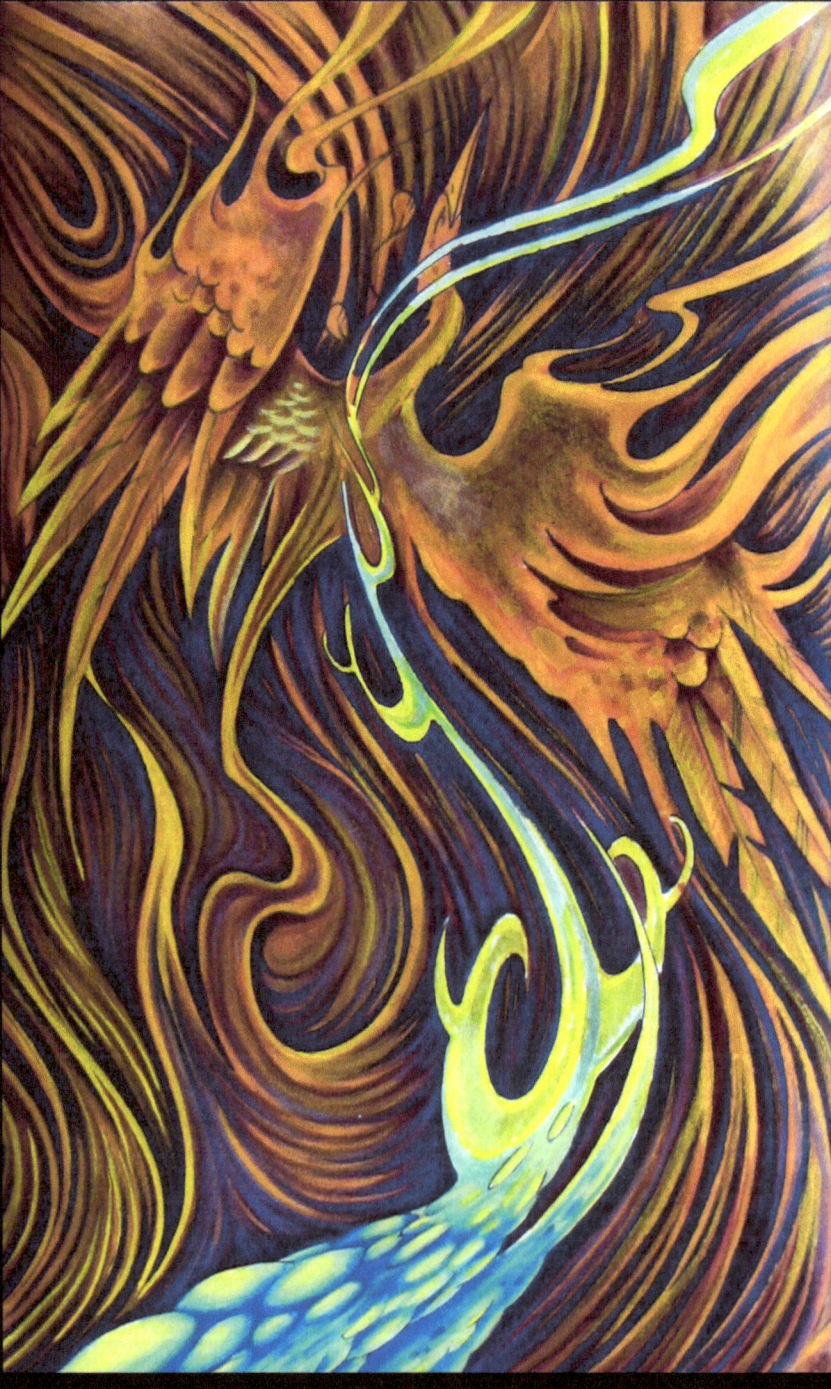

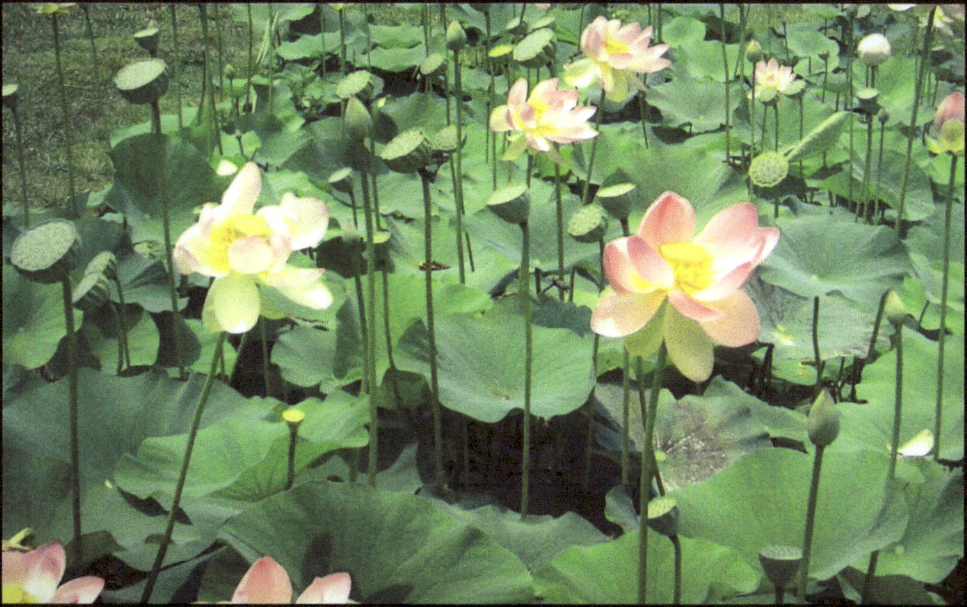

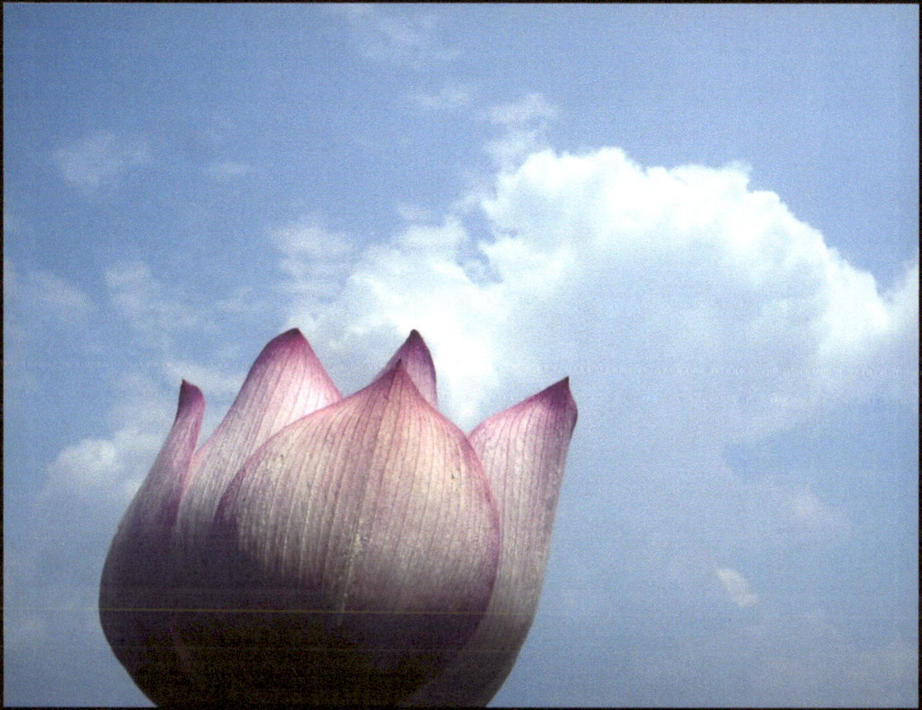

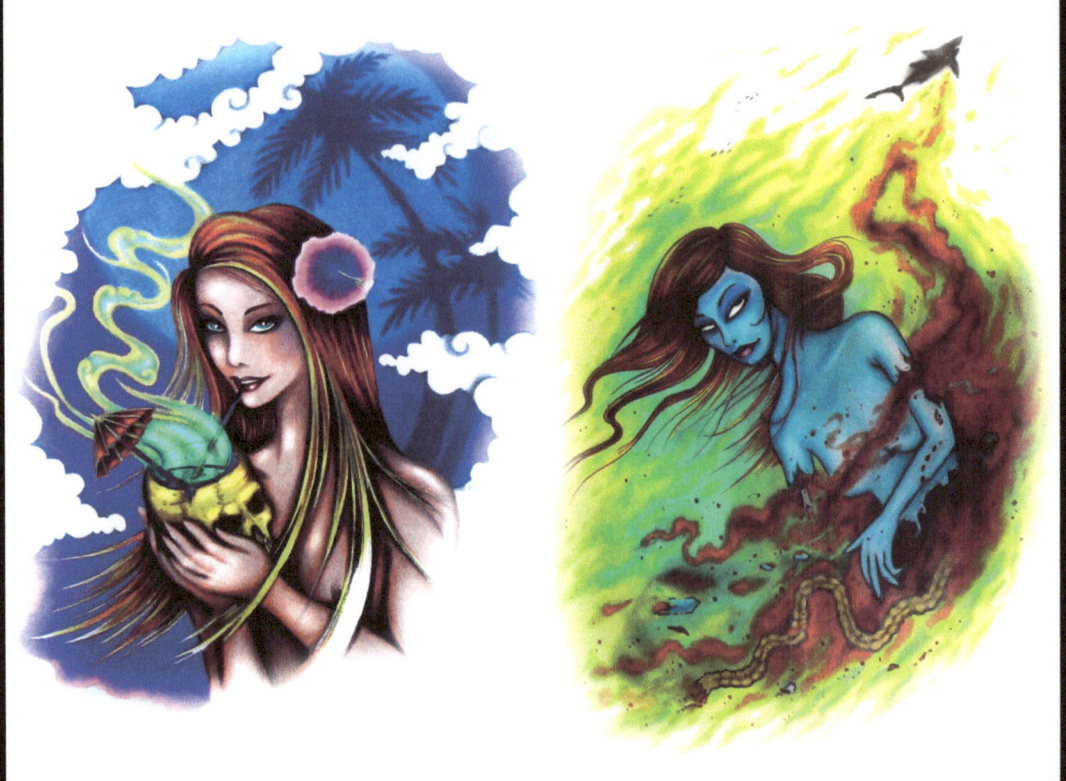
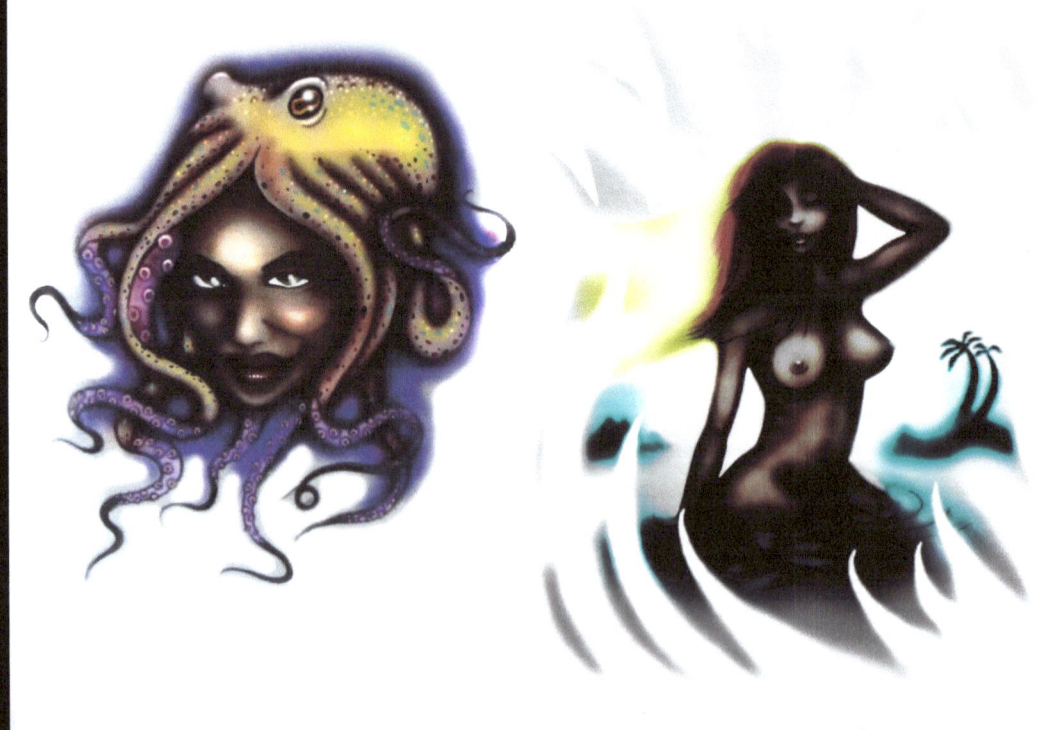

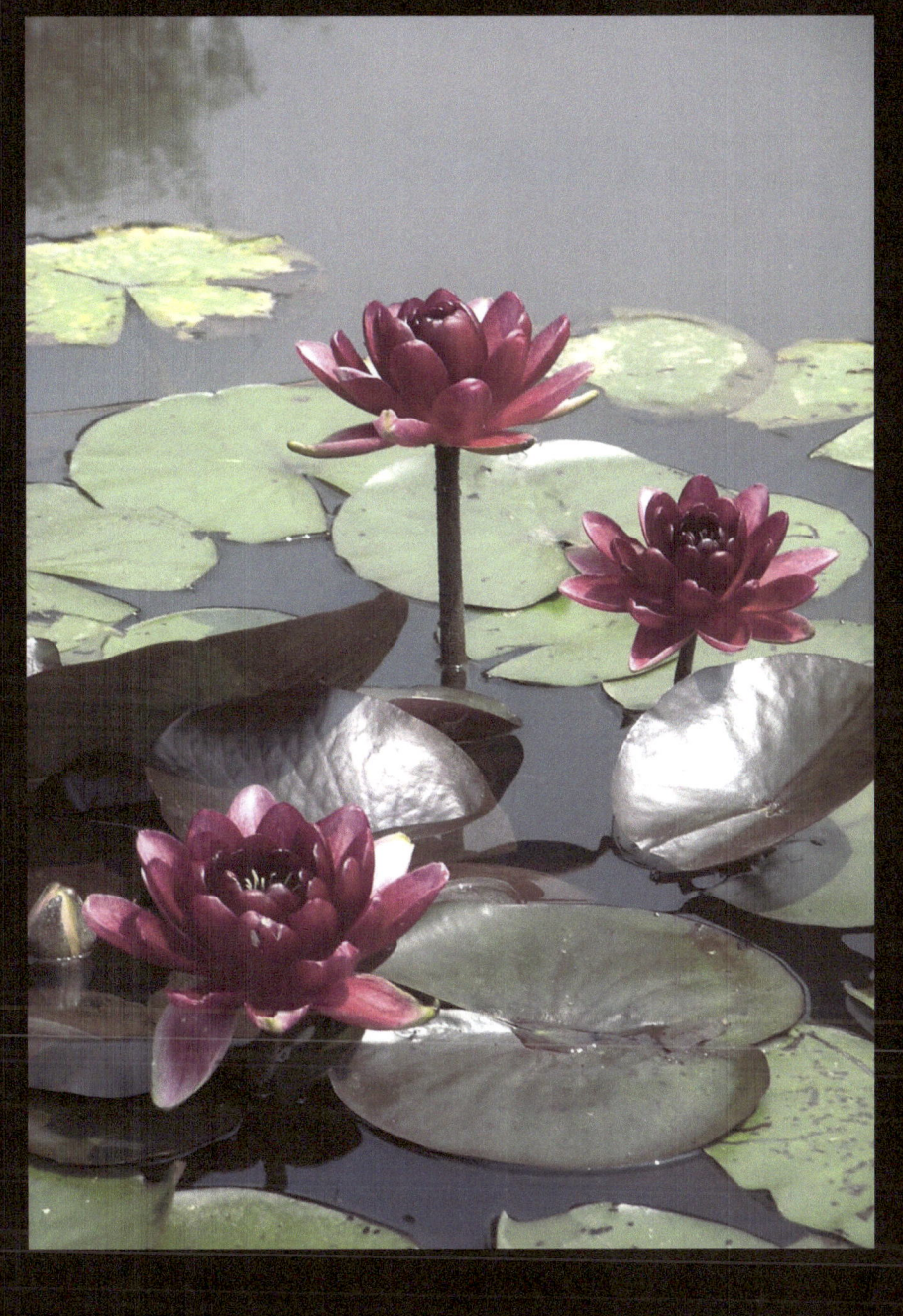

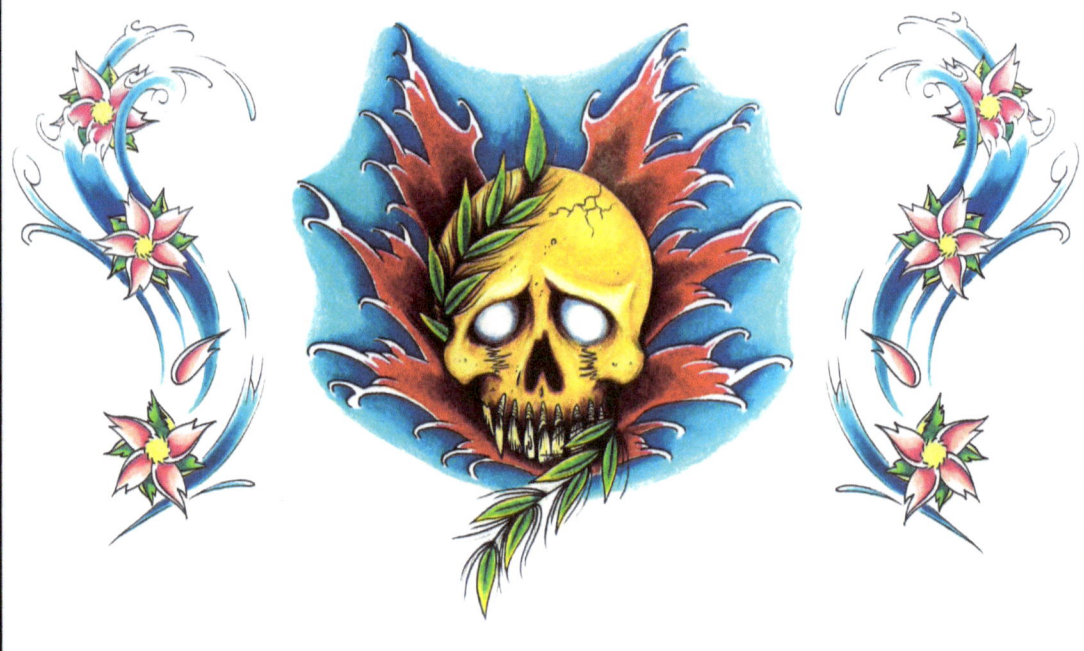

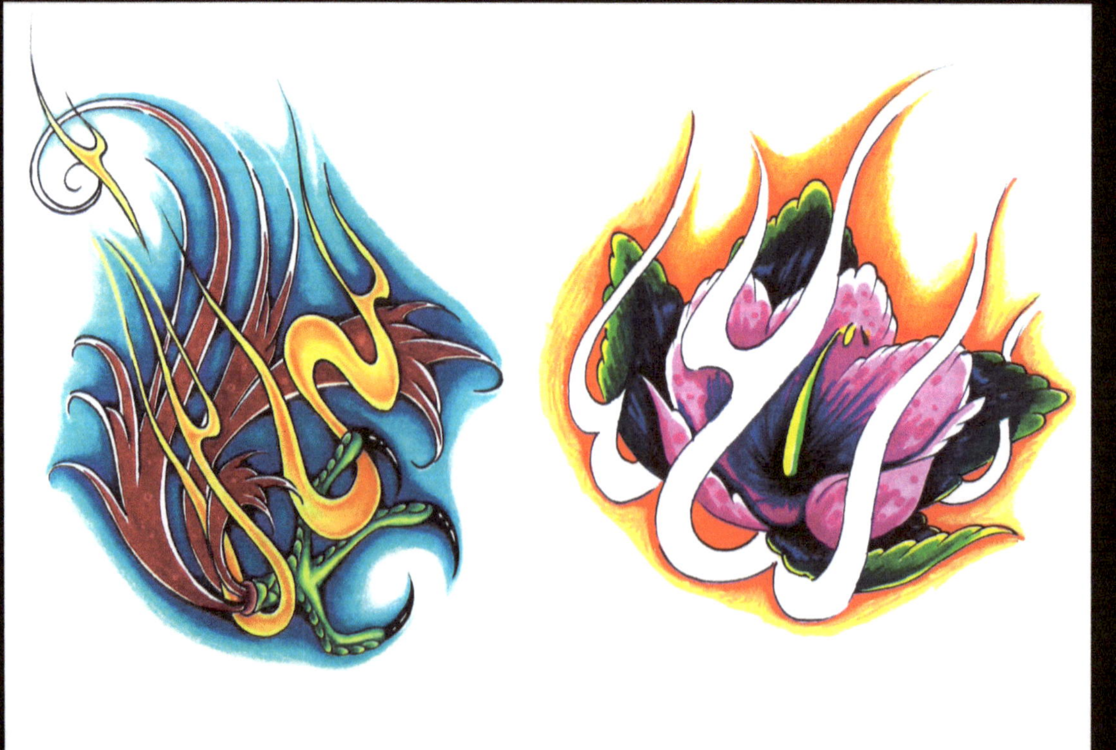

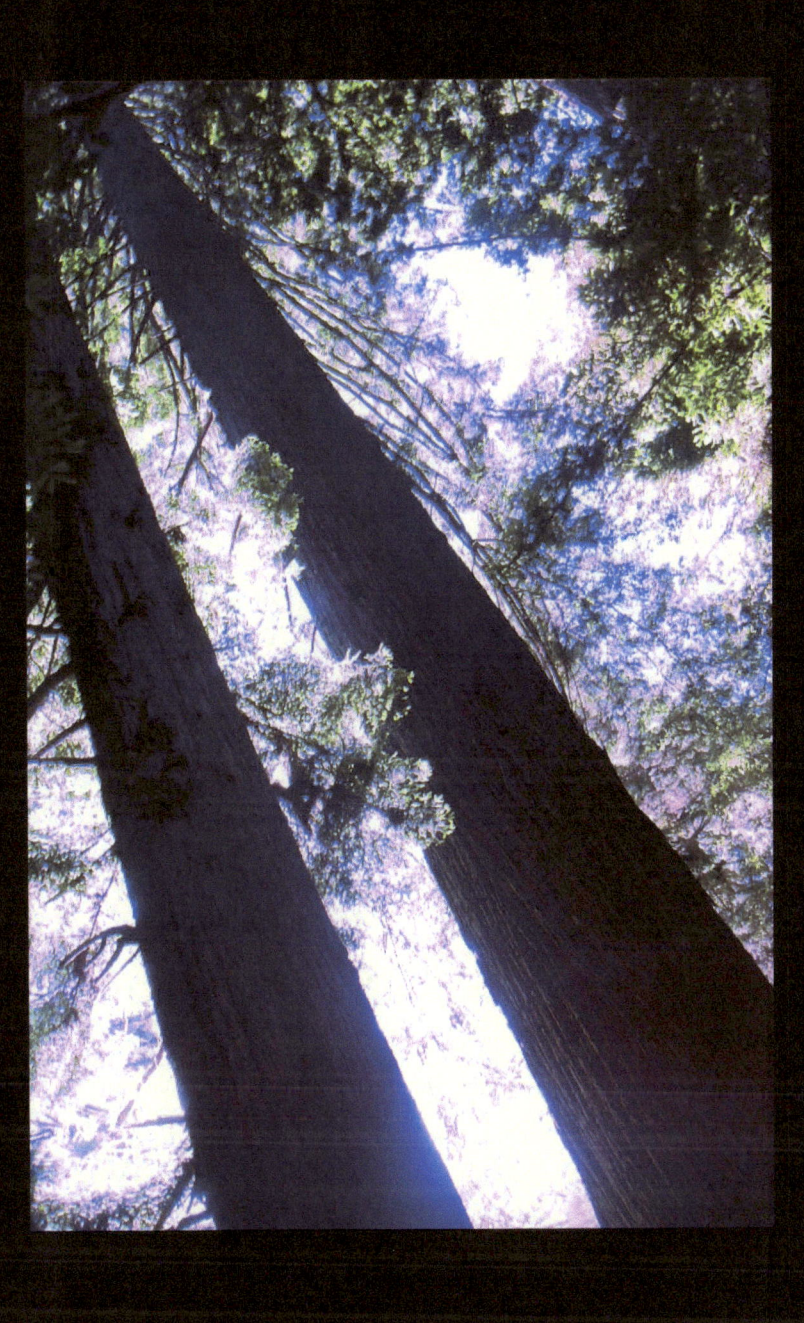

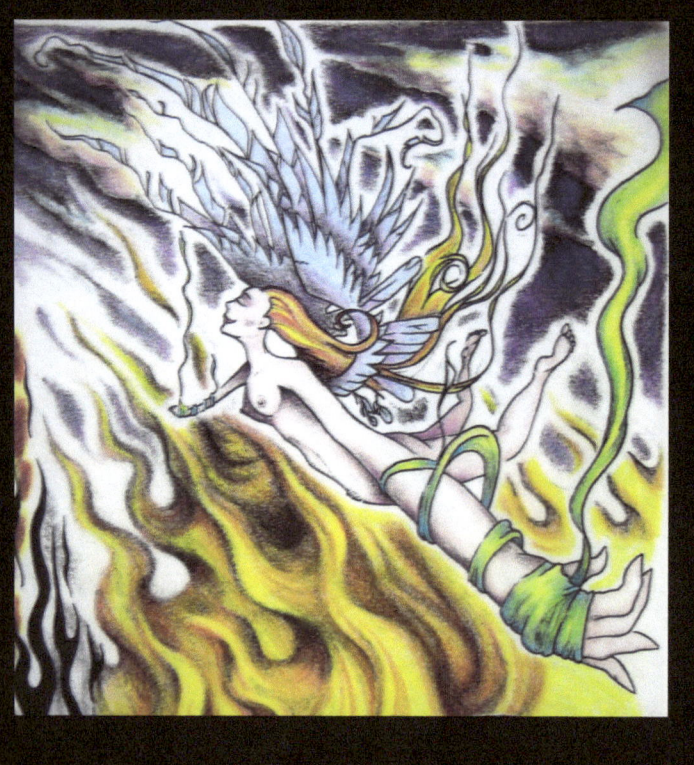
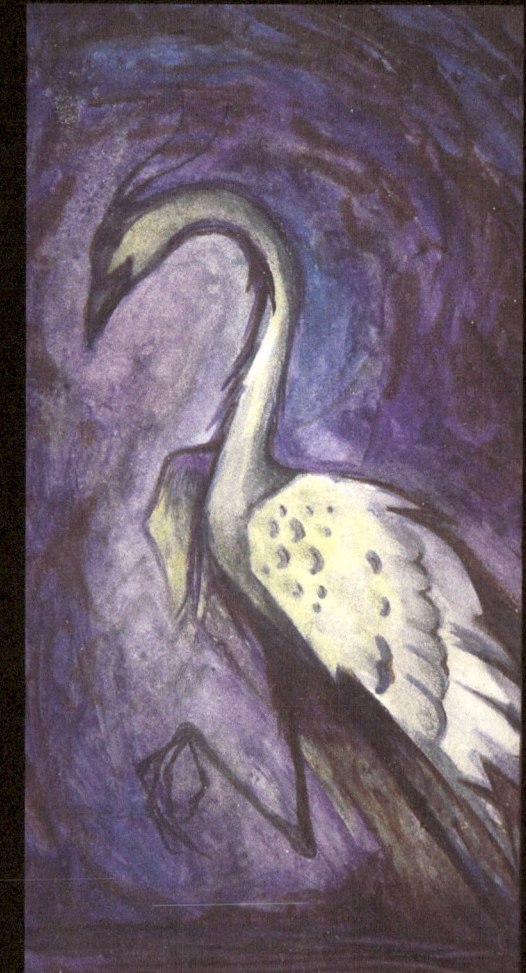
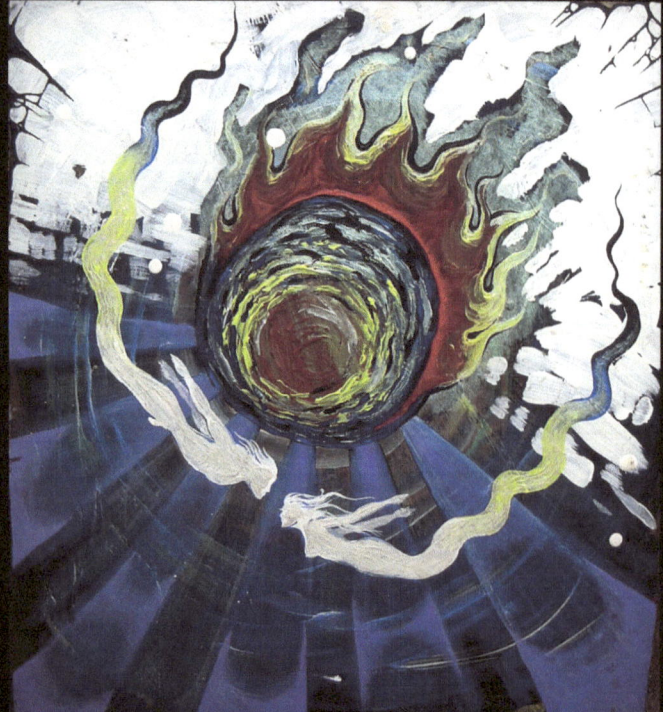
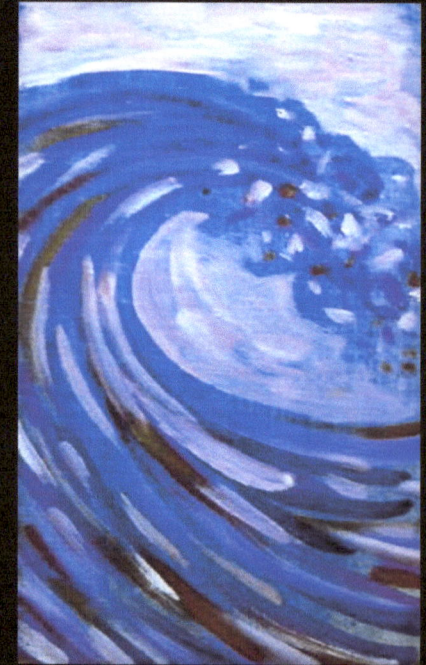

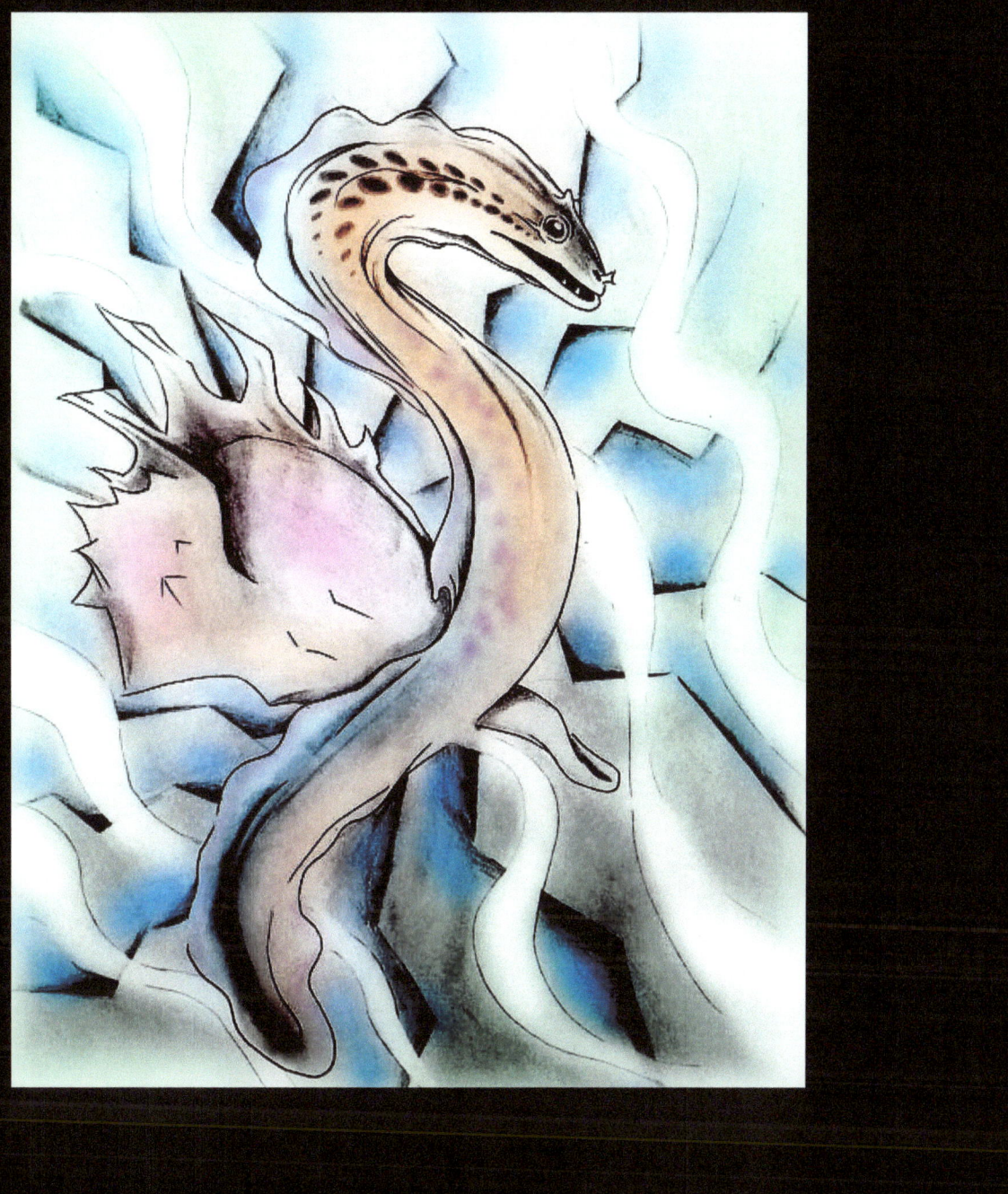

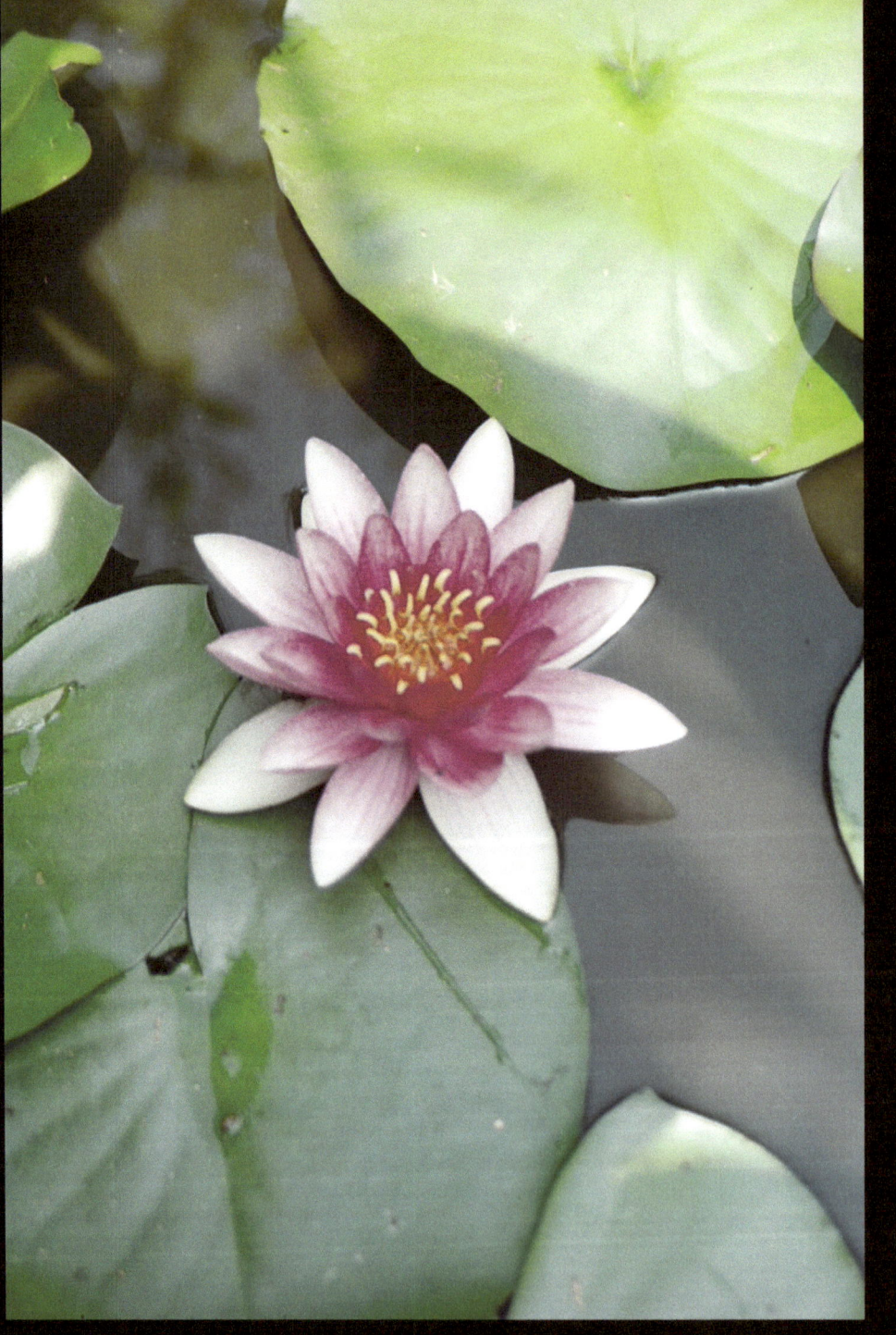

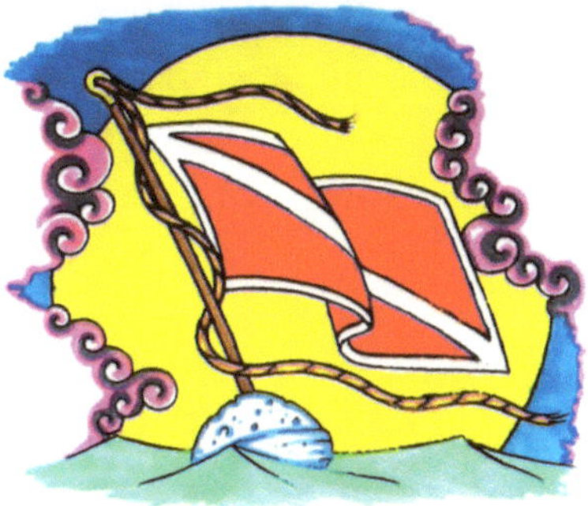
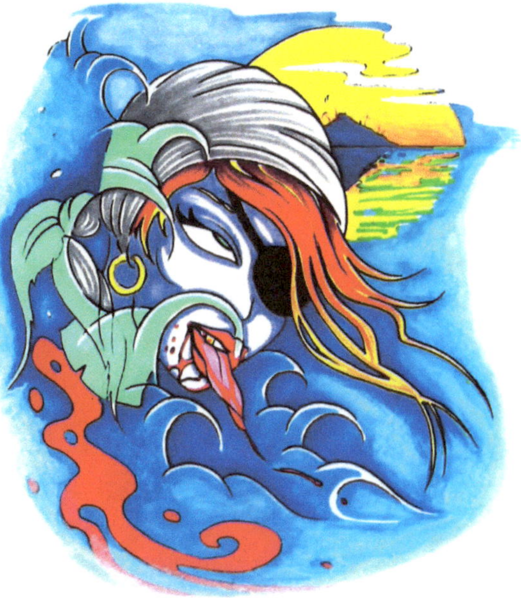
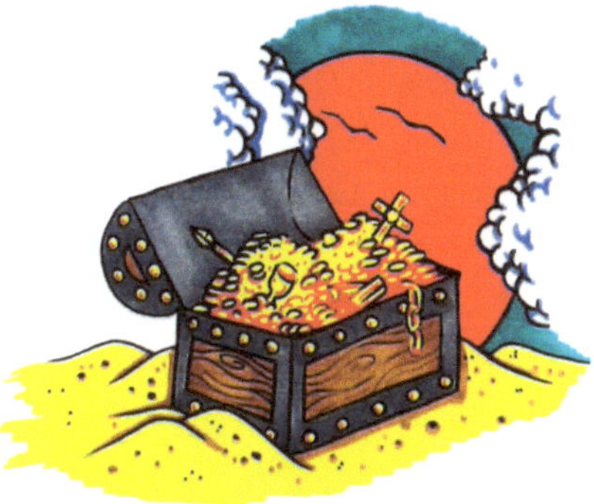
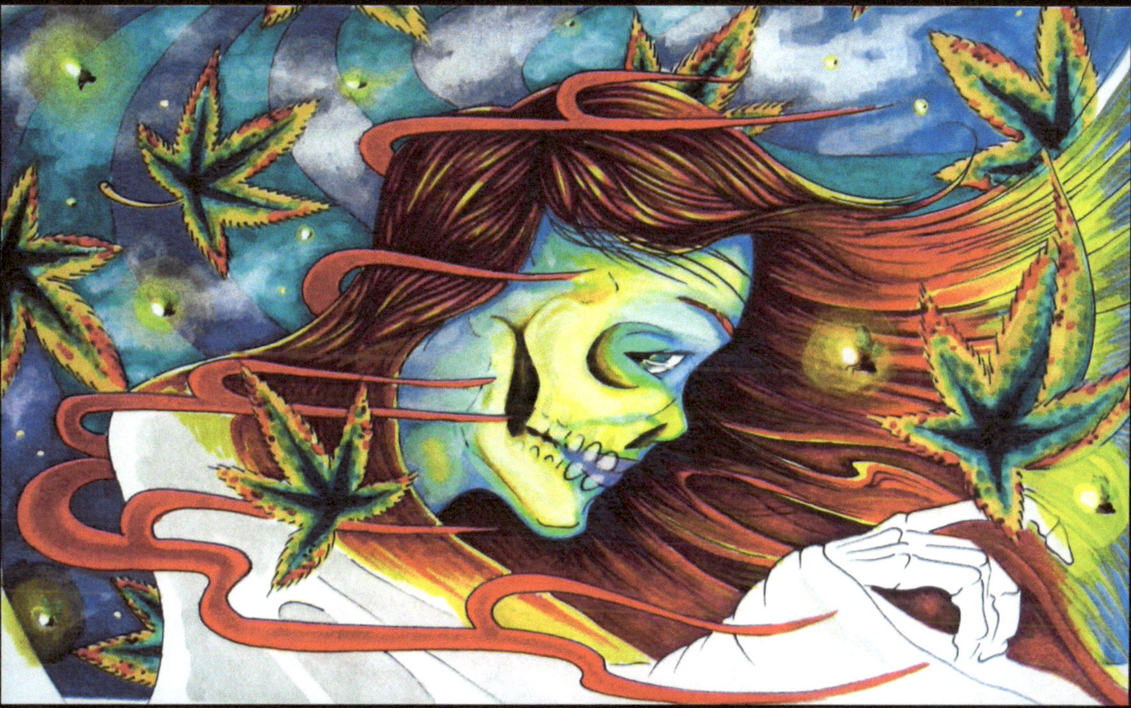

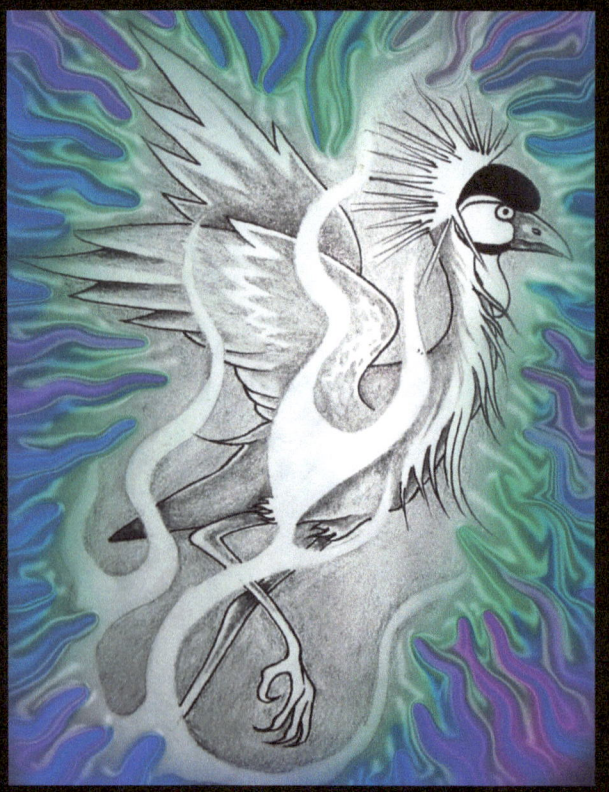

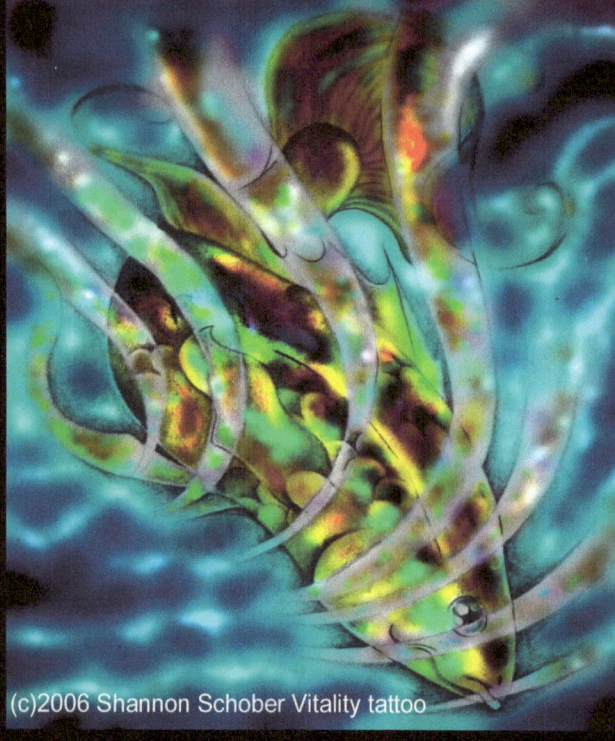

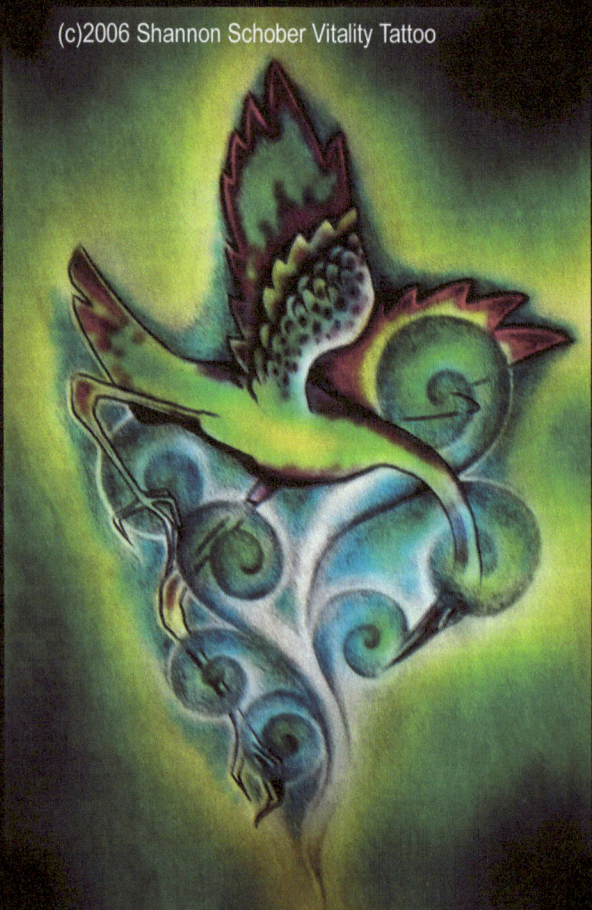

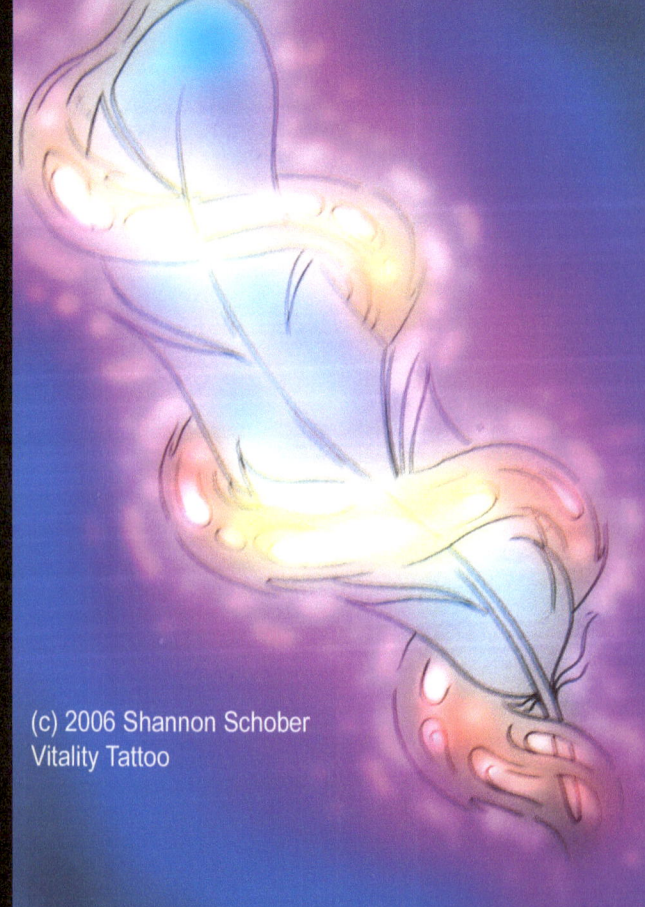

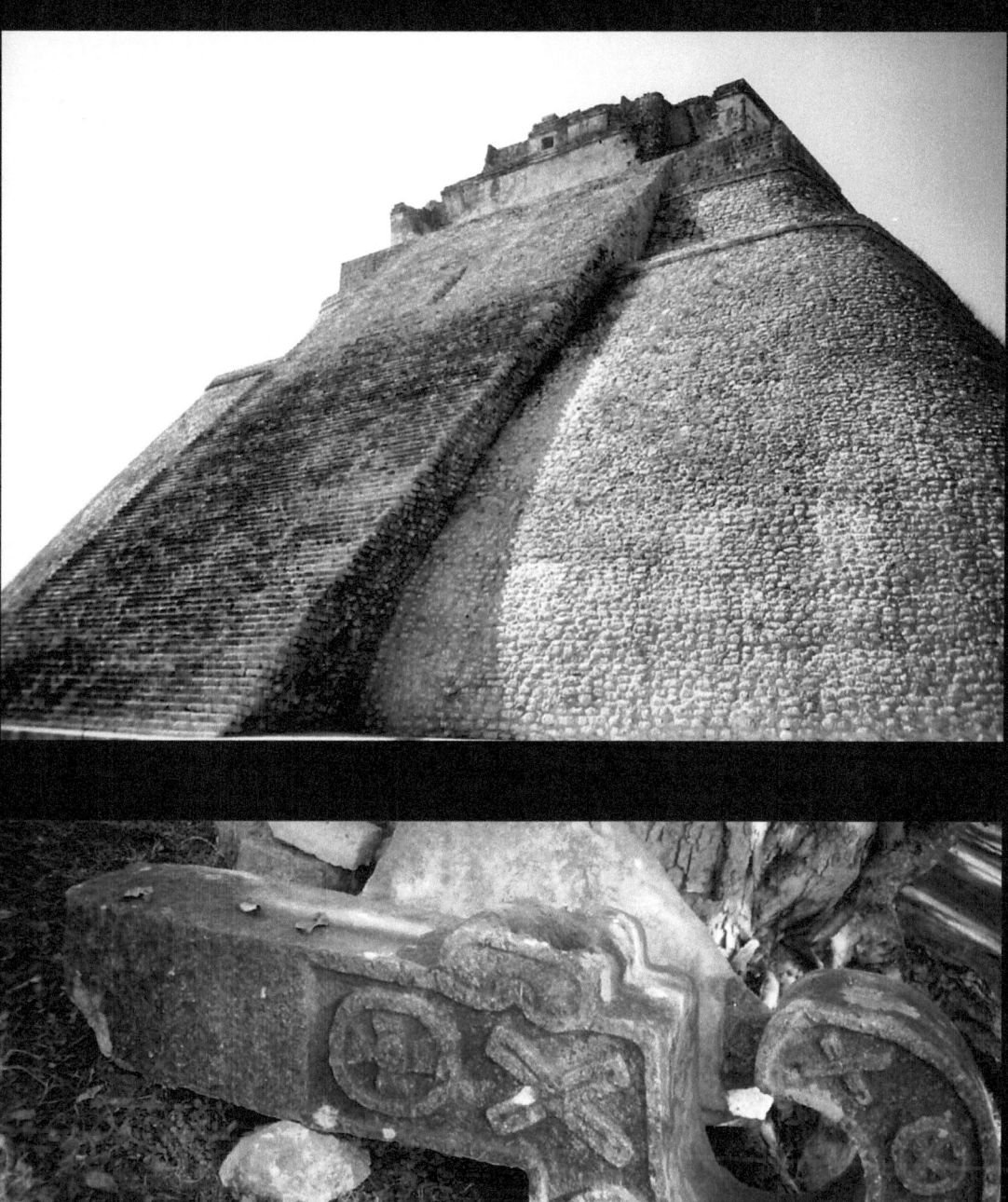

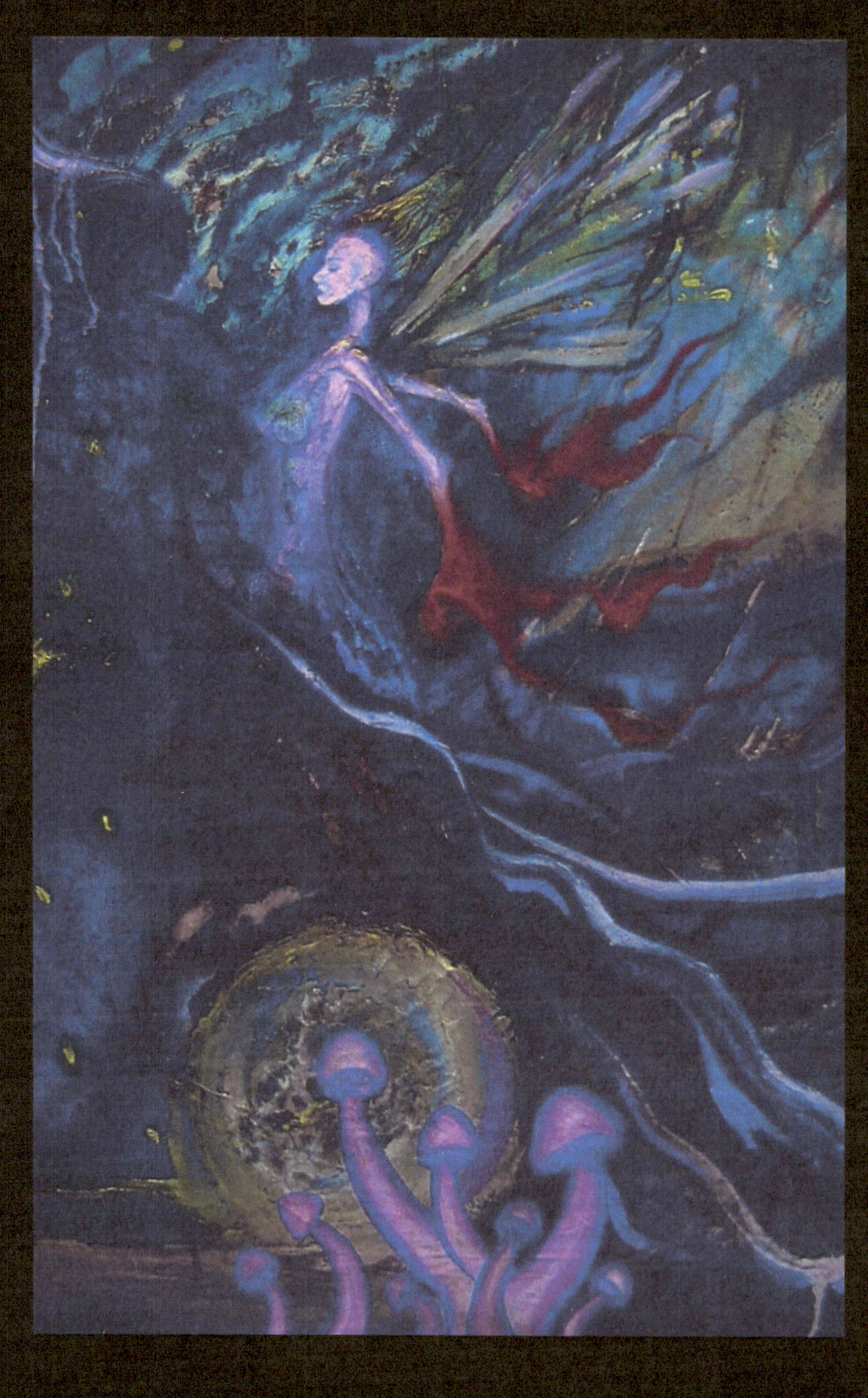

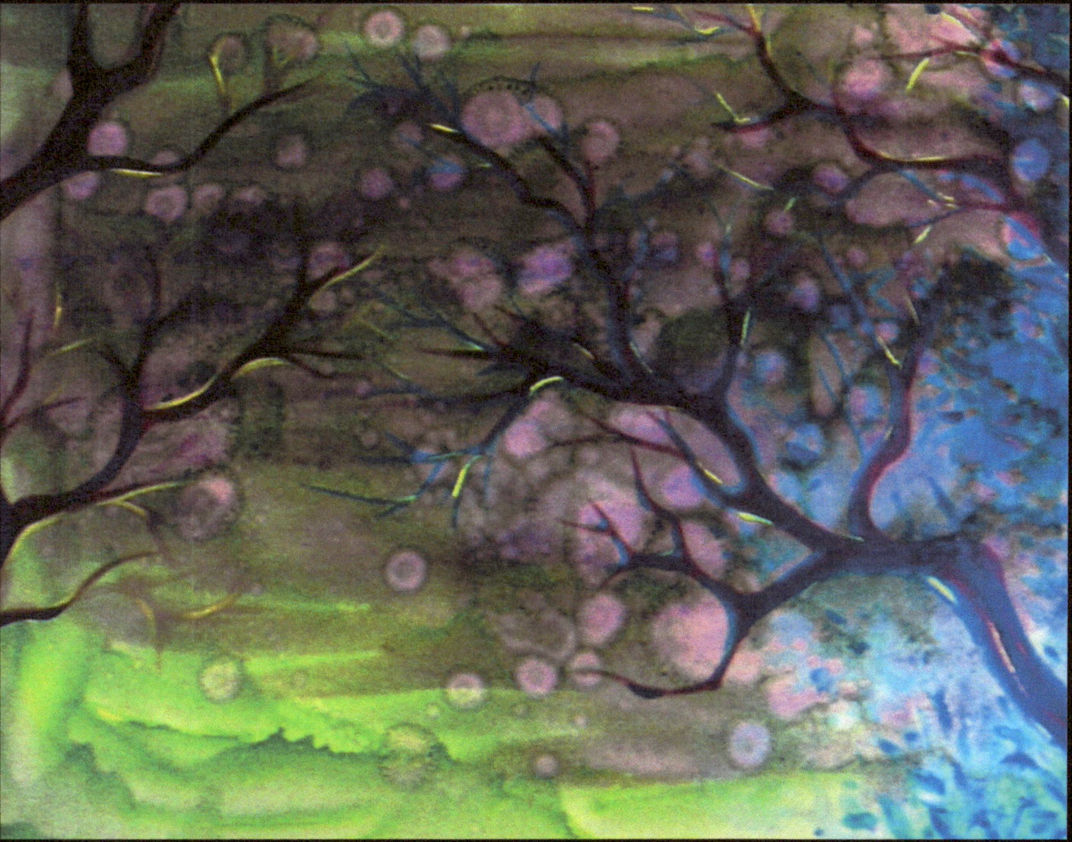

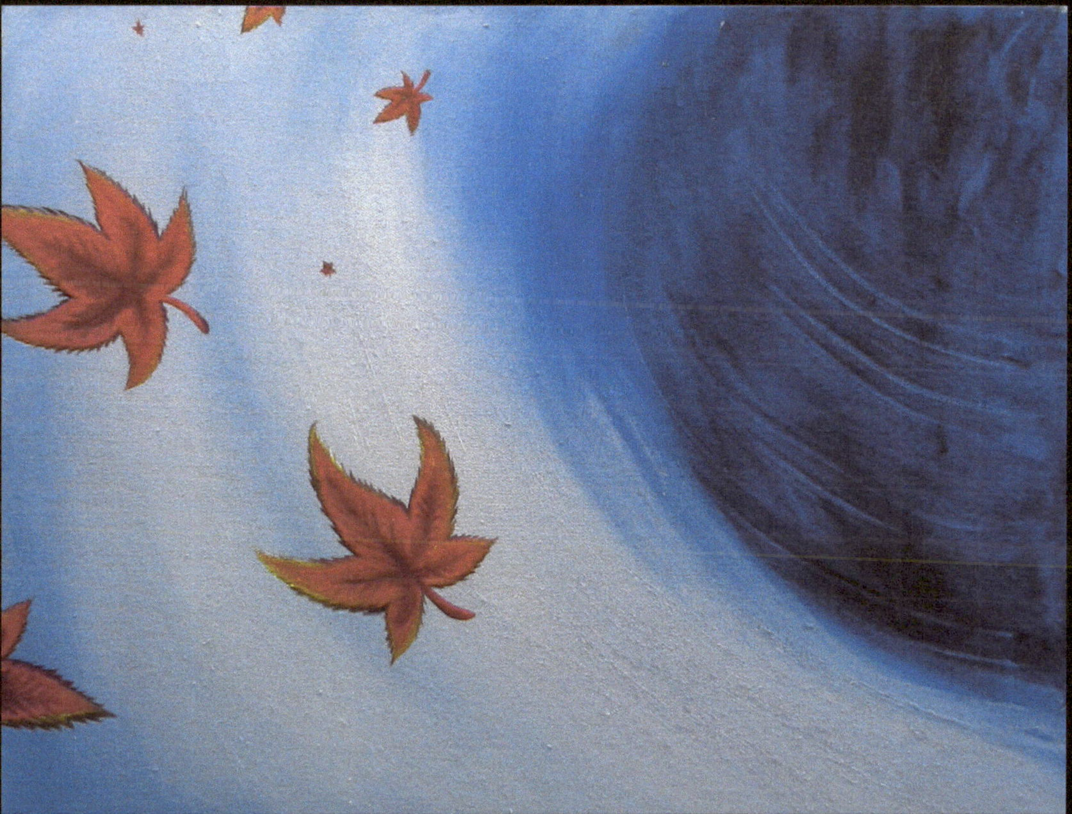

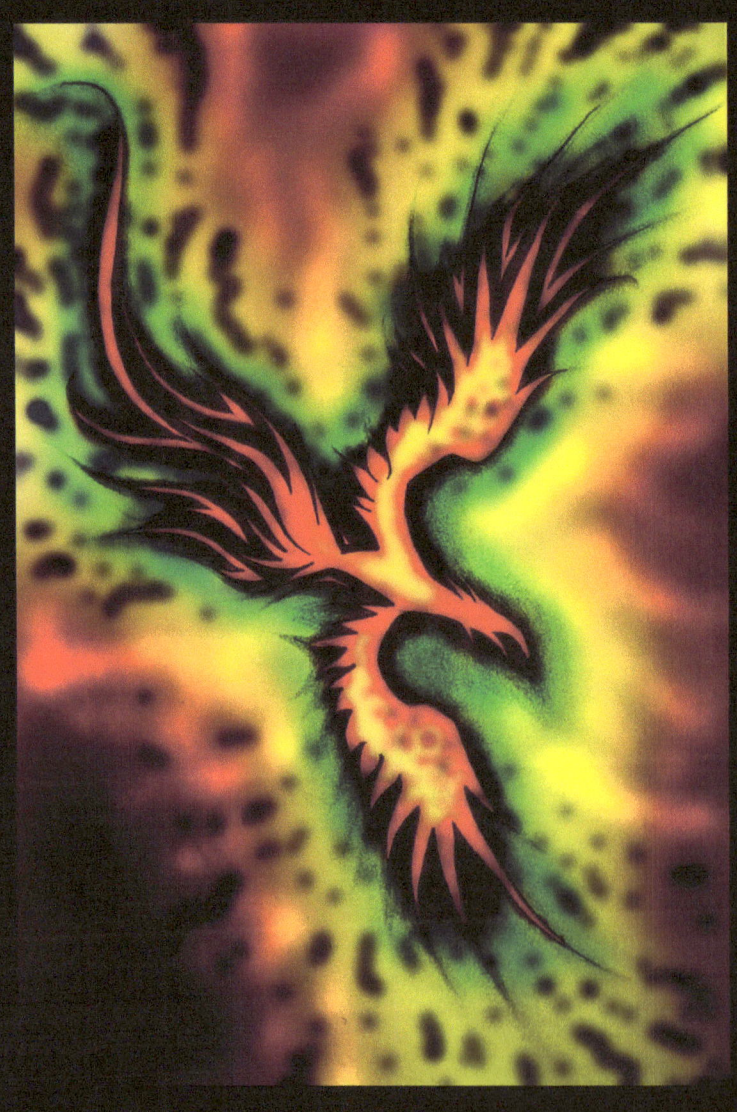

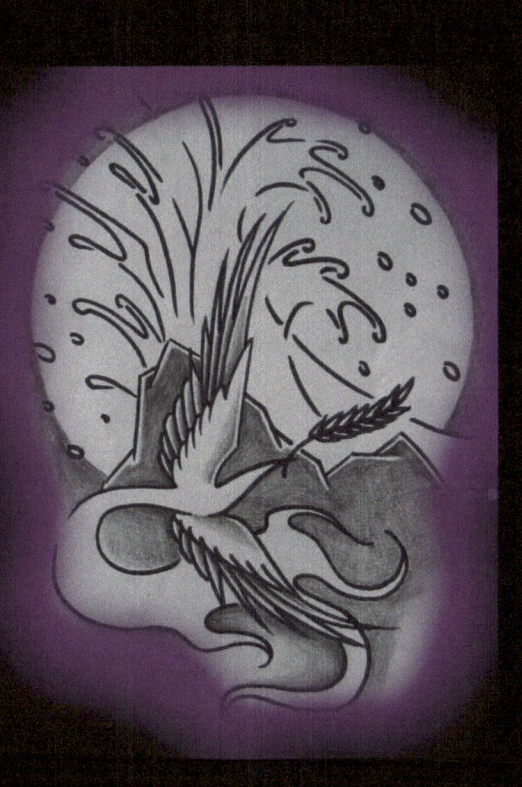

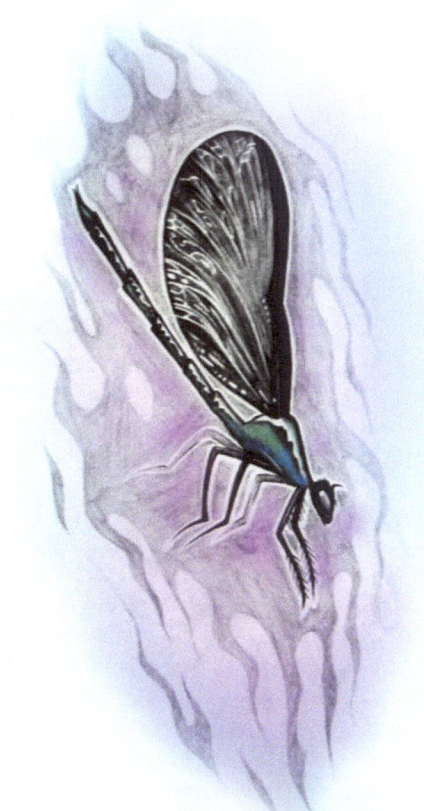

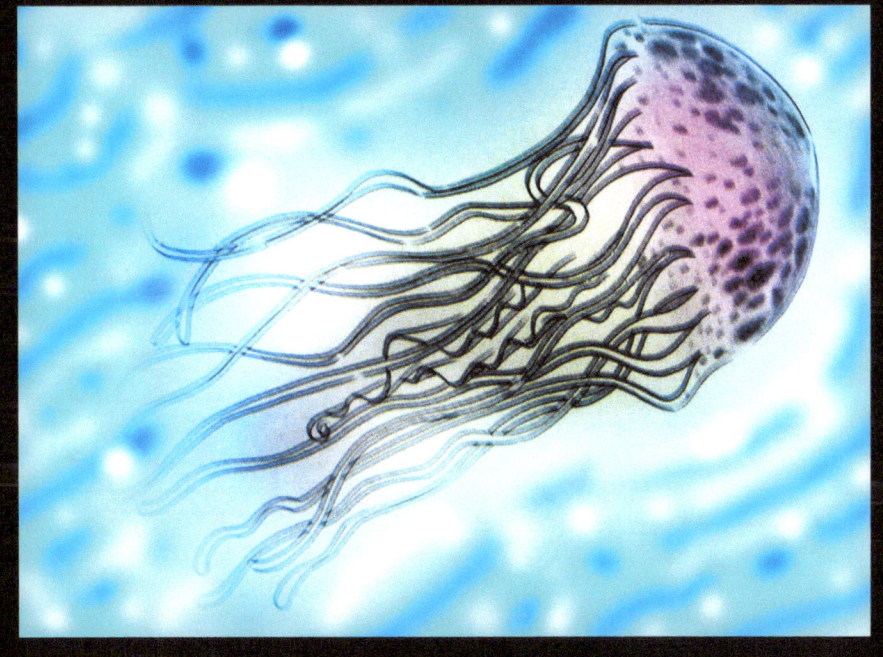

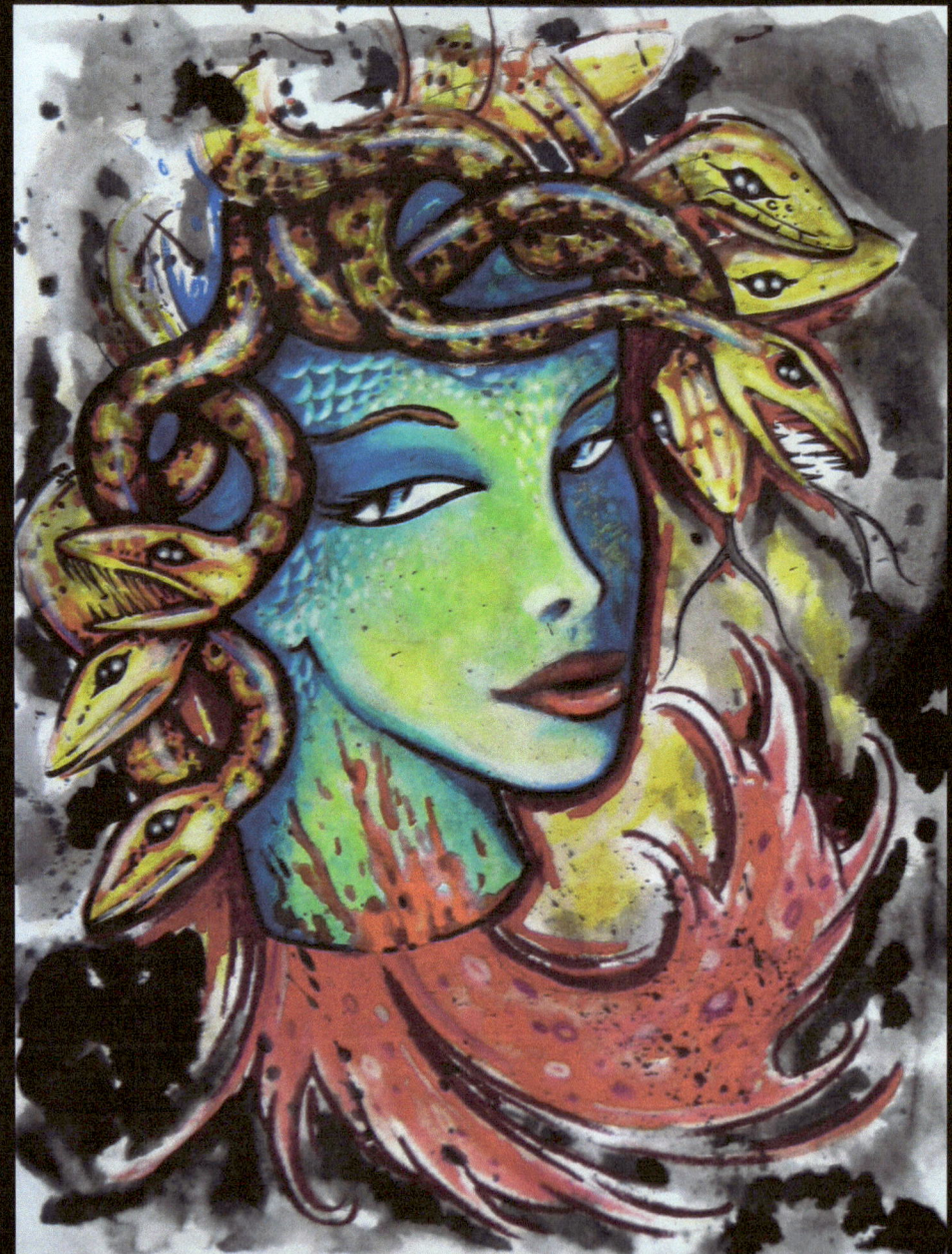

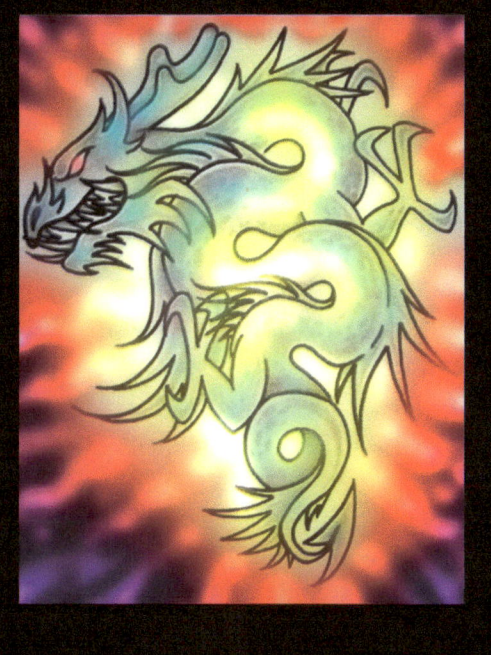
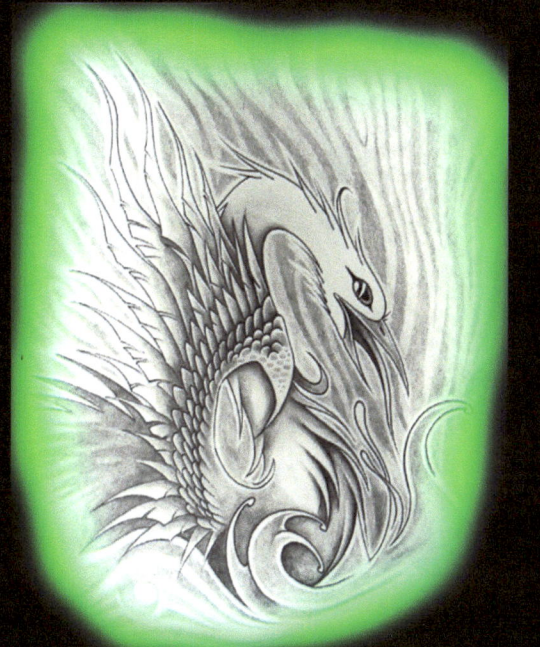
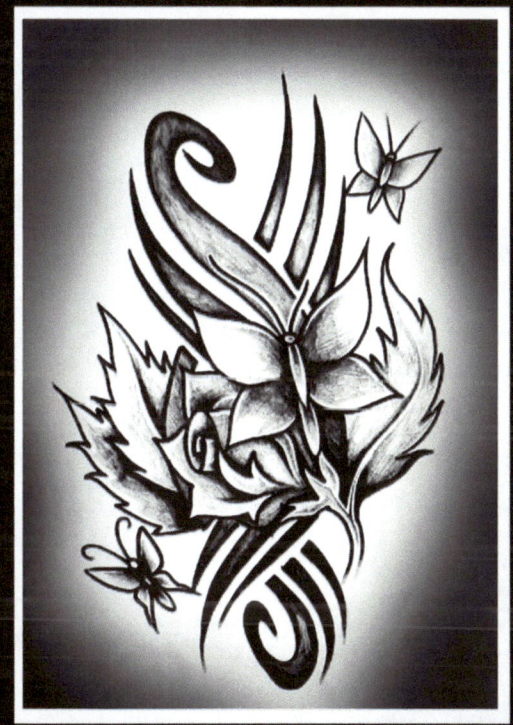
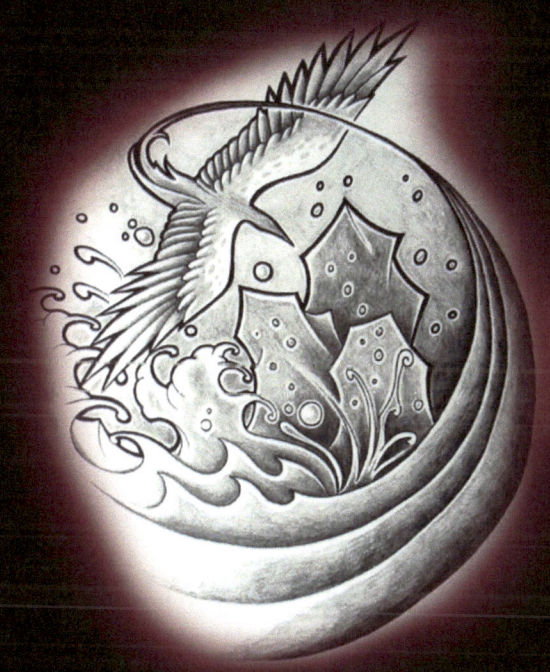

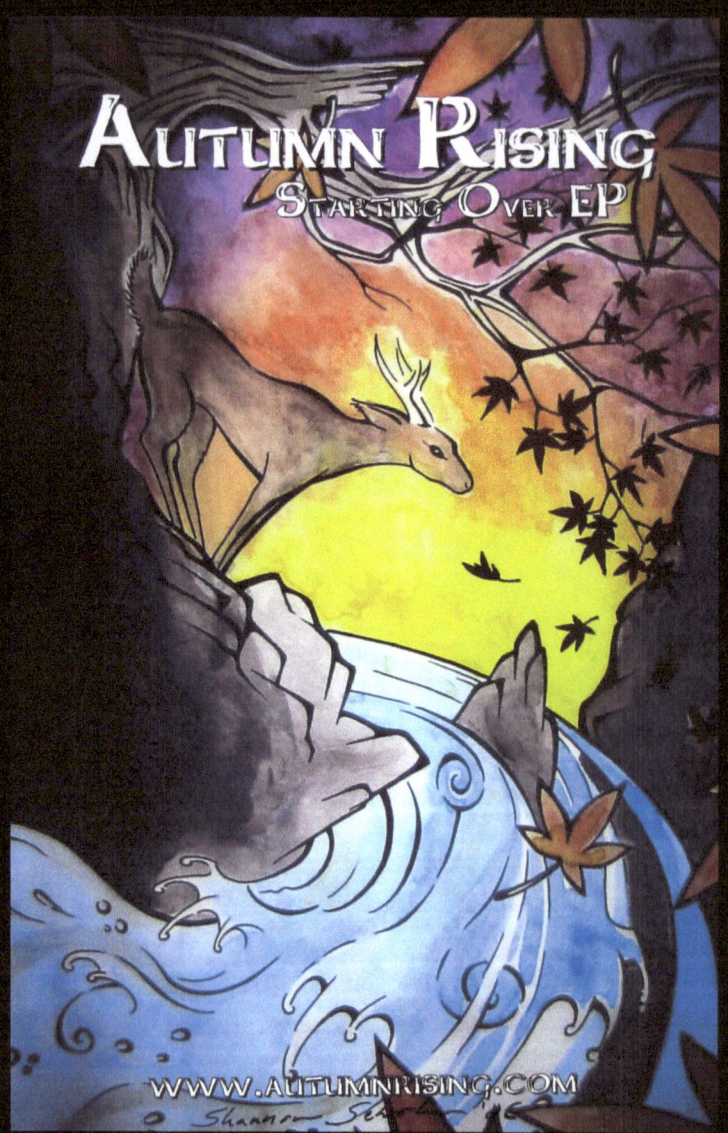

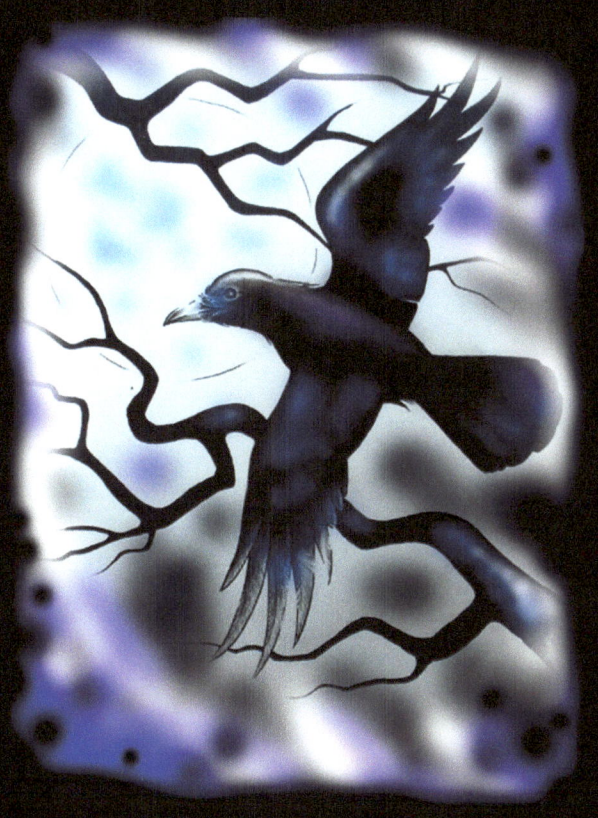

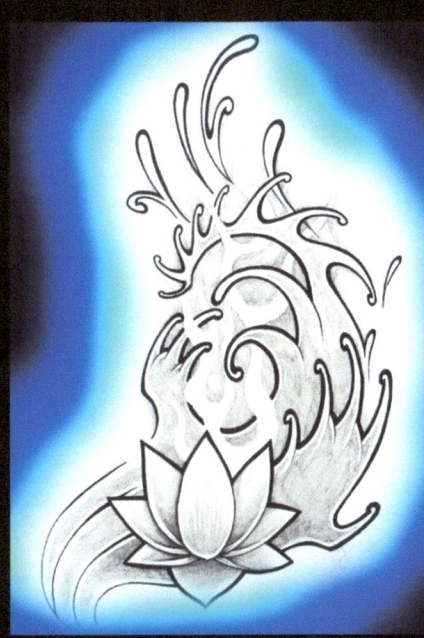

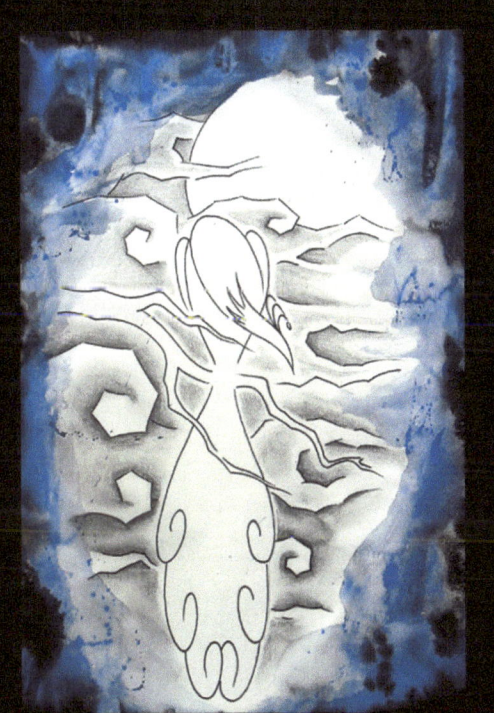

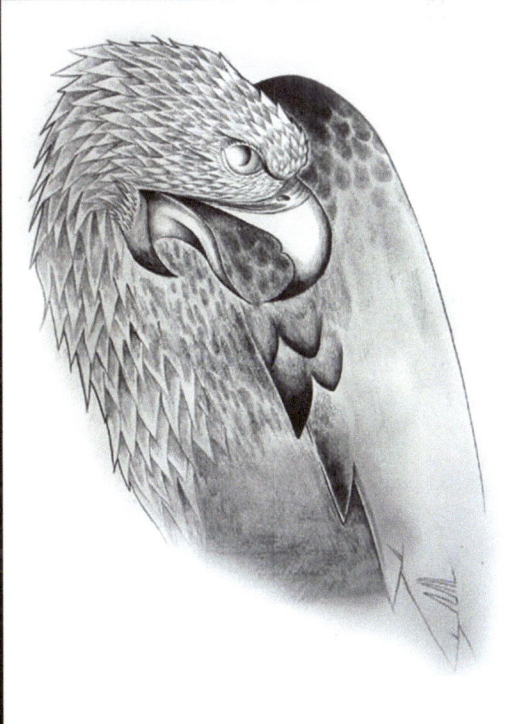

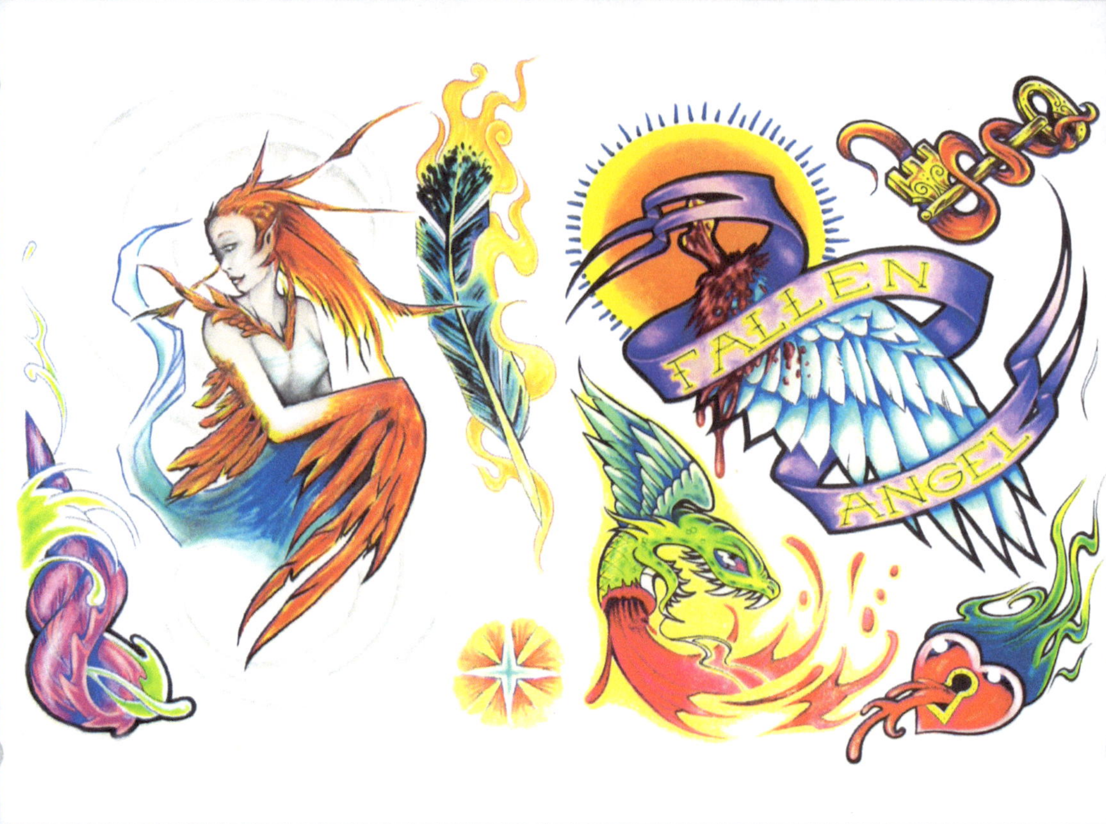
FALLEN
ANGEL

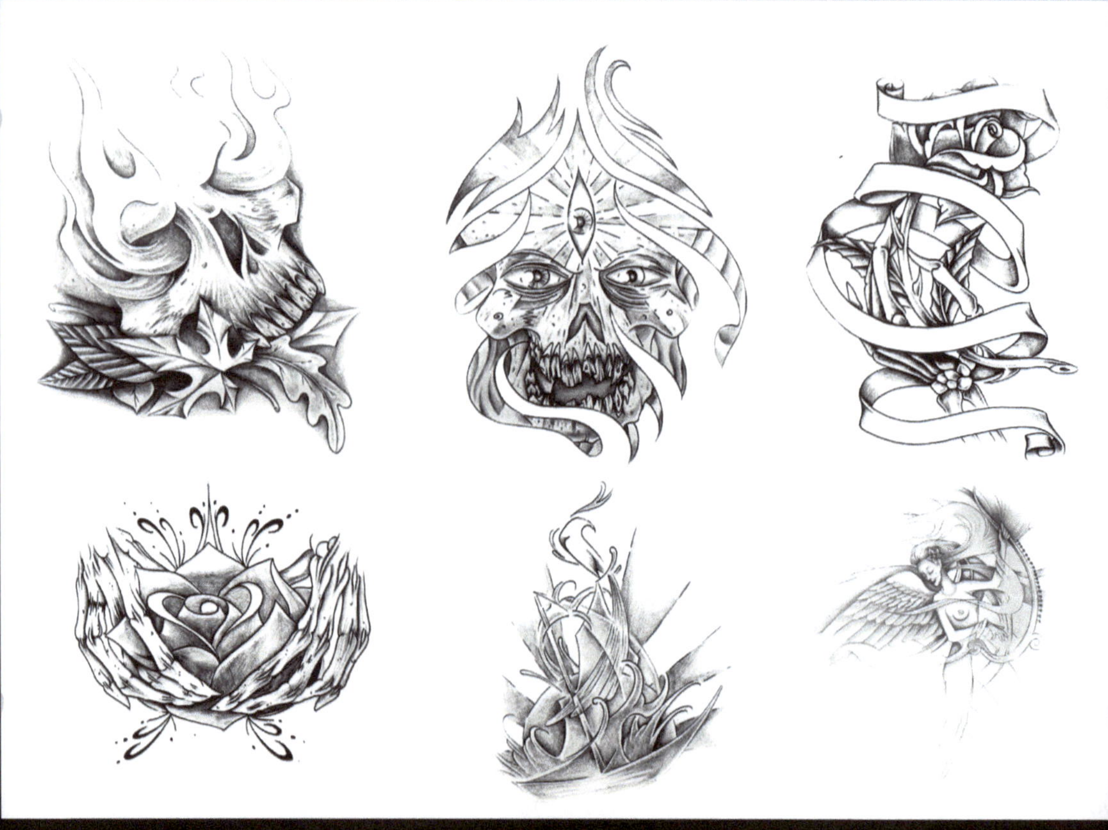

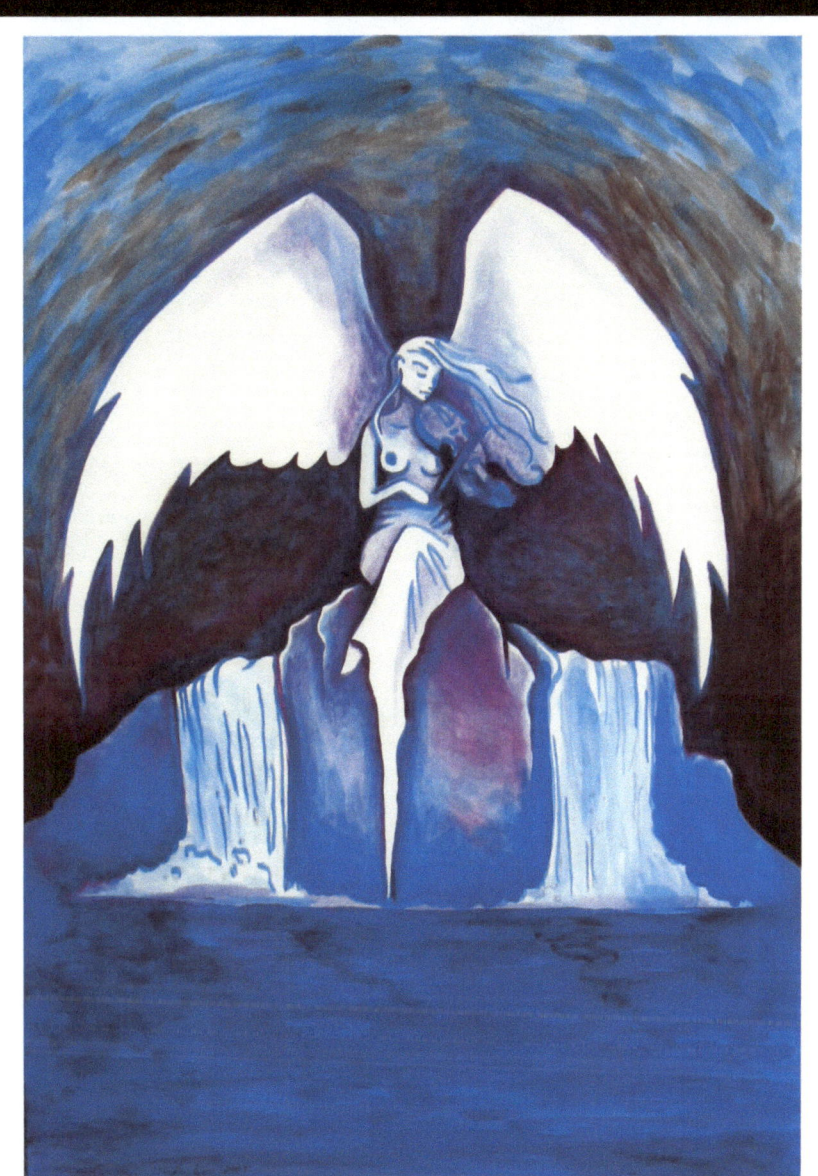

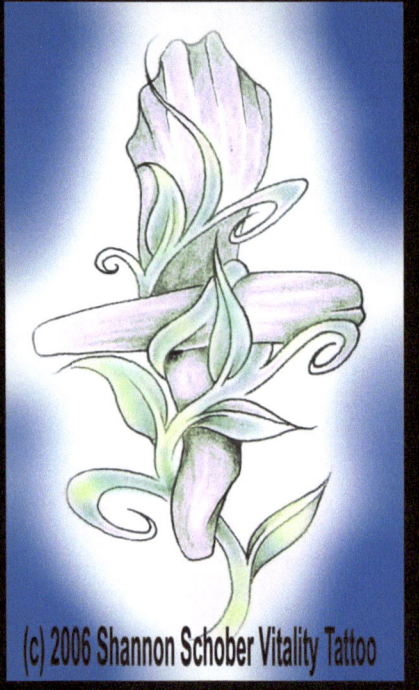

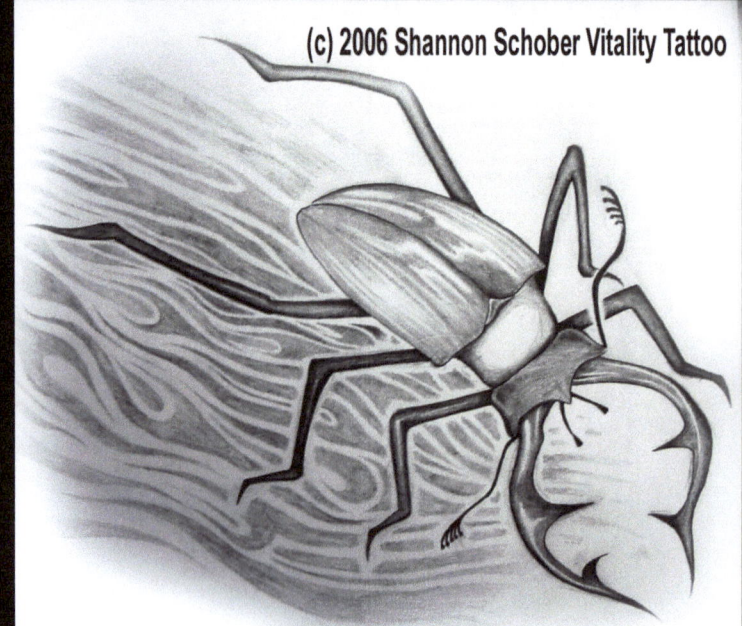

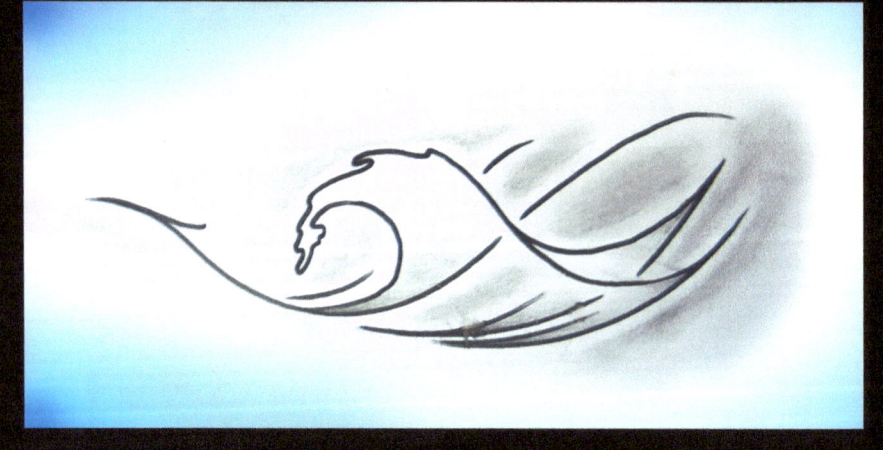

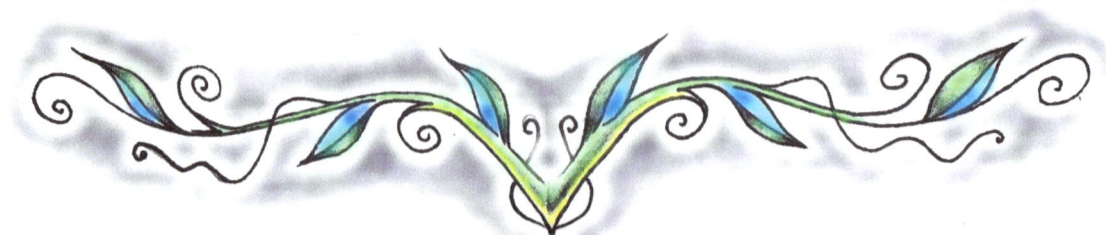

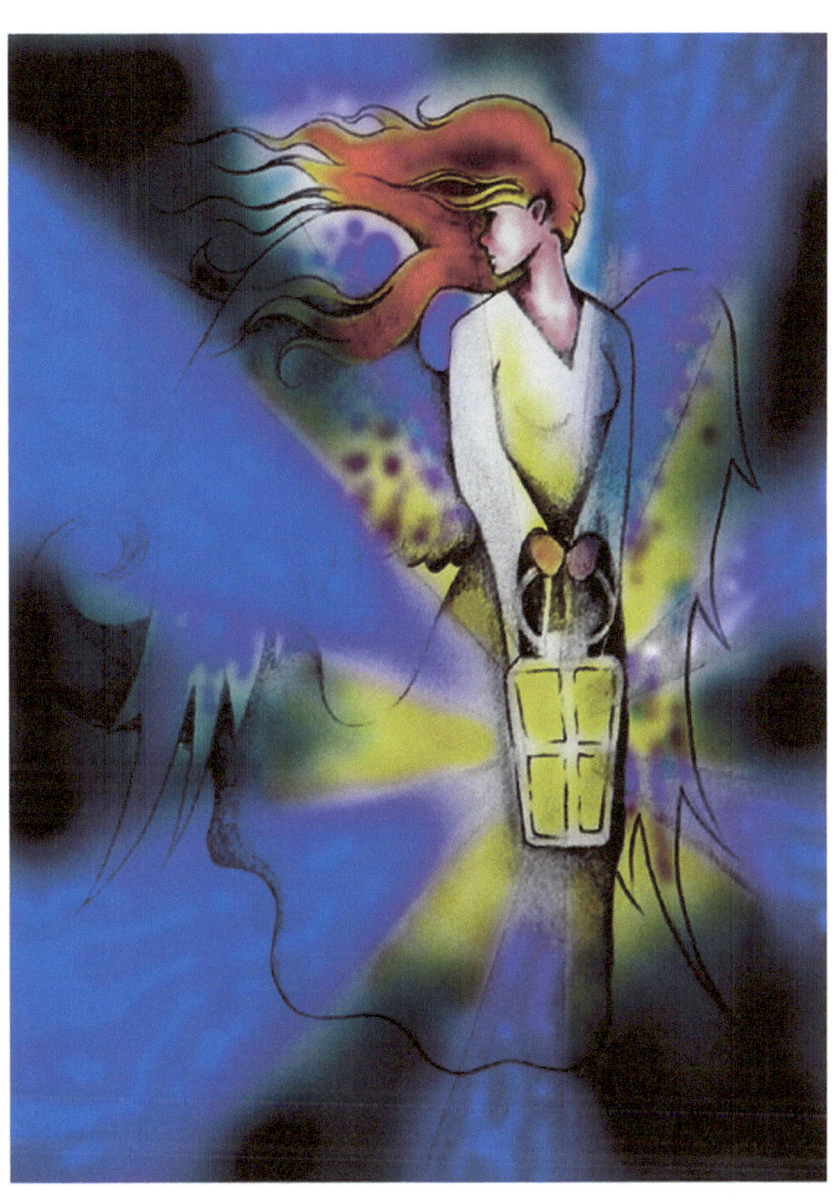

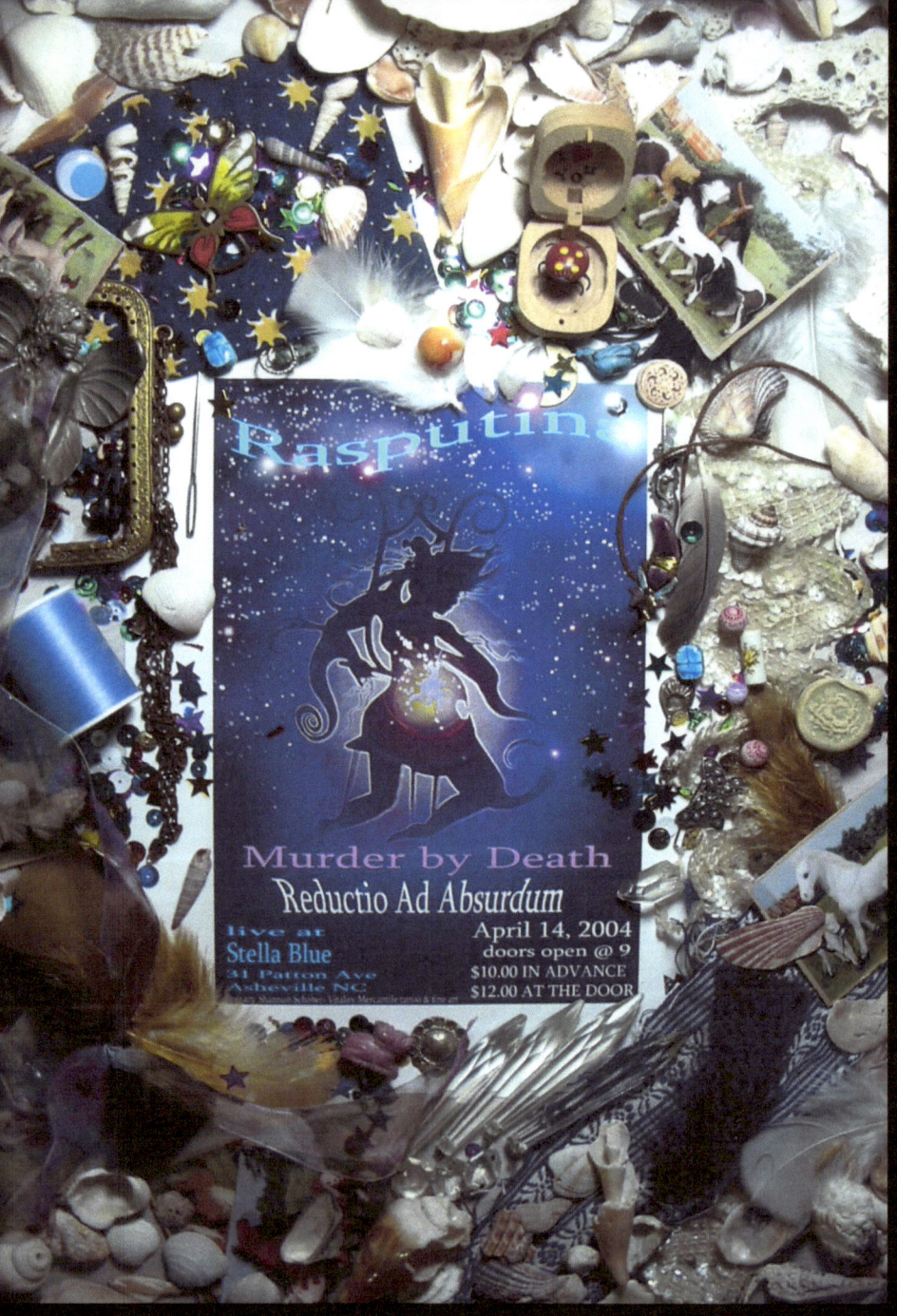

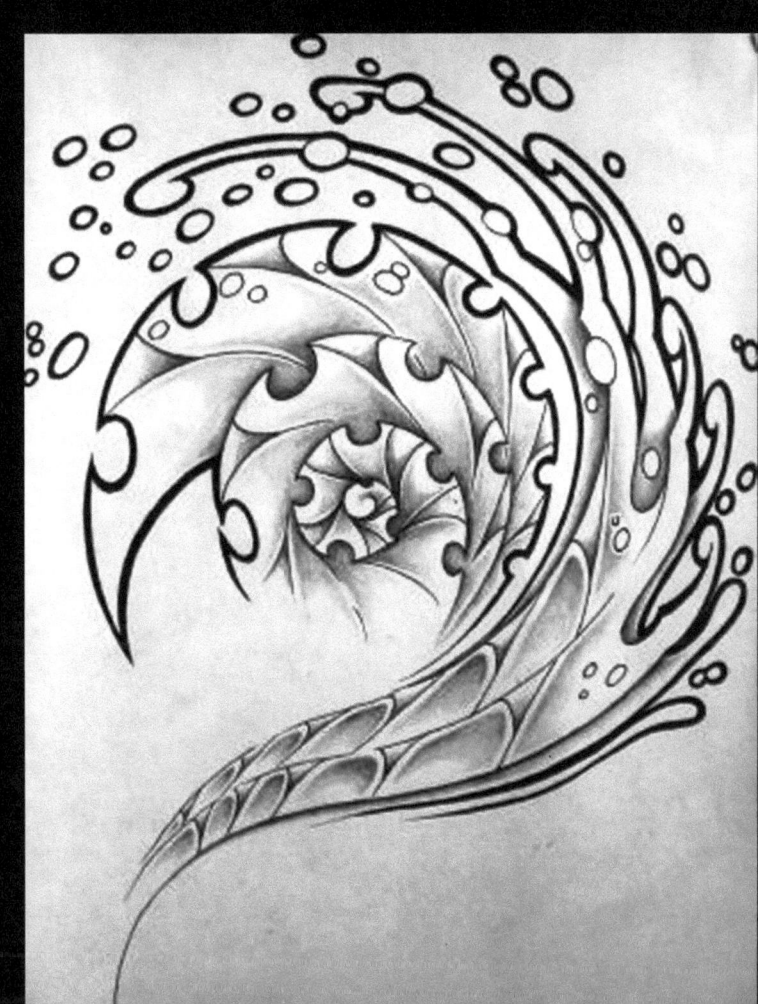

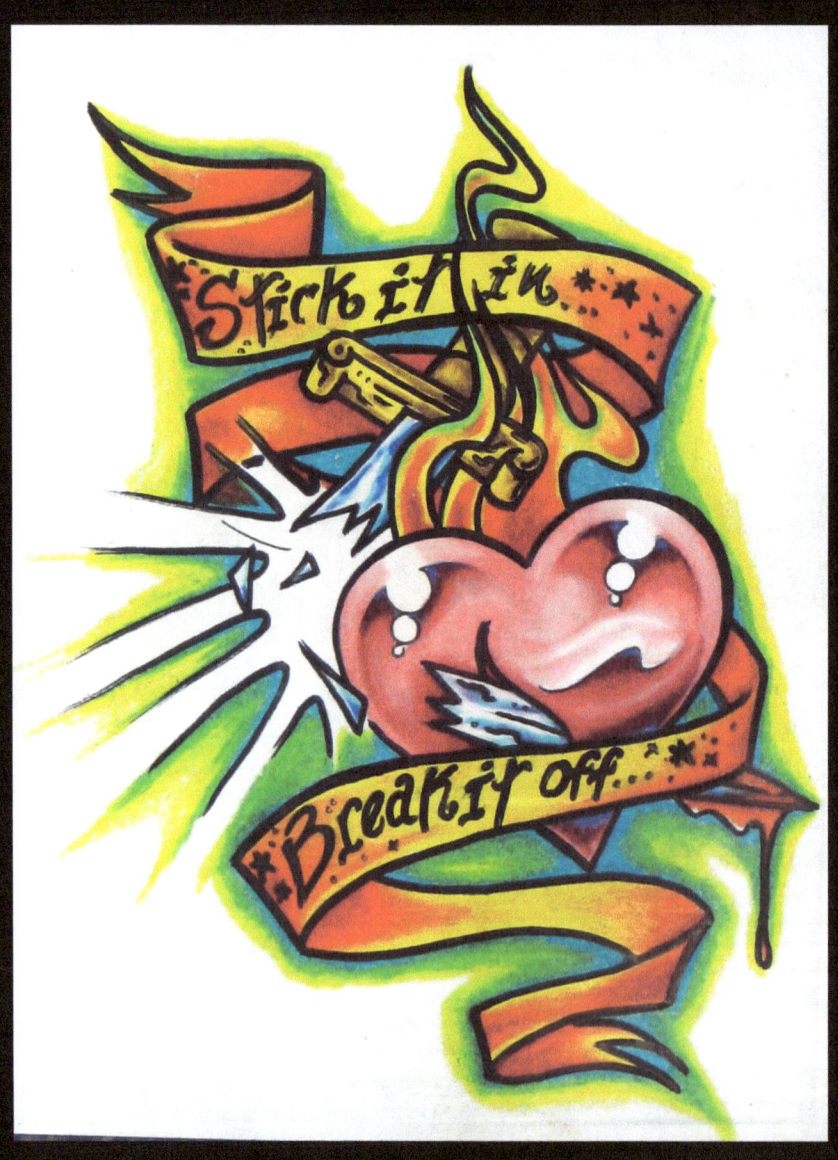

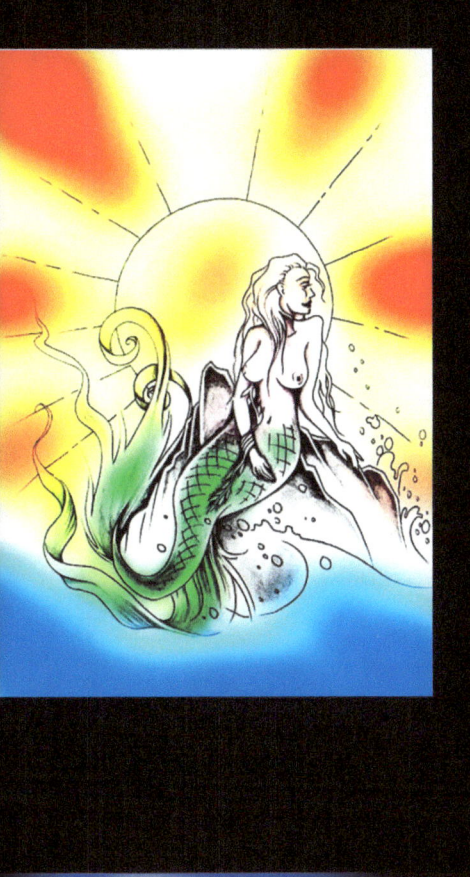
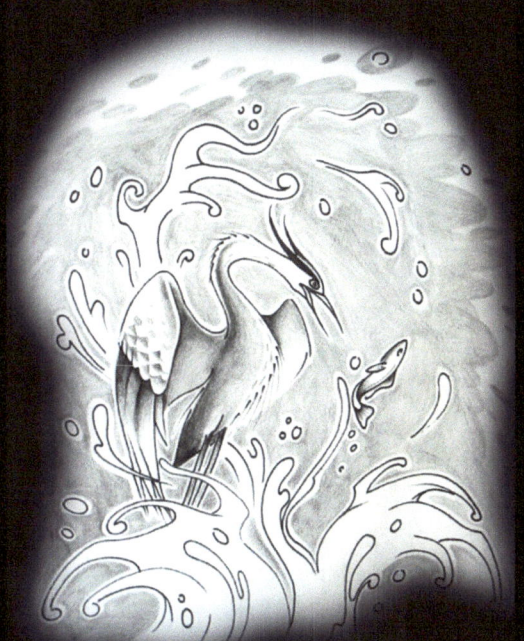
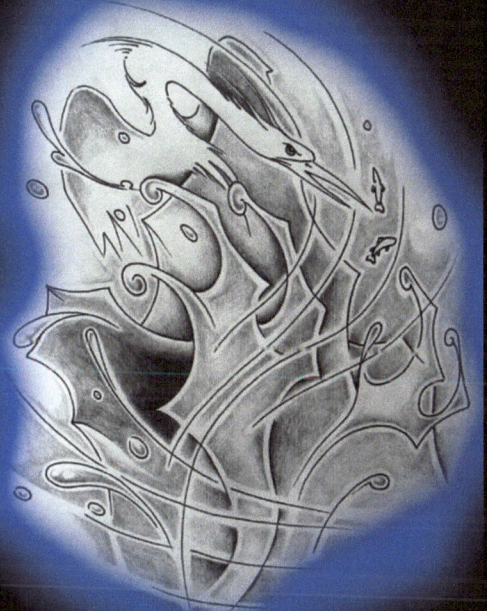
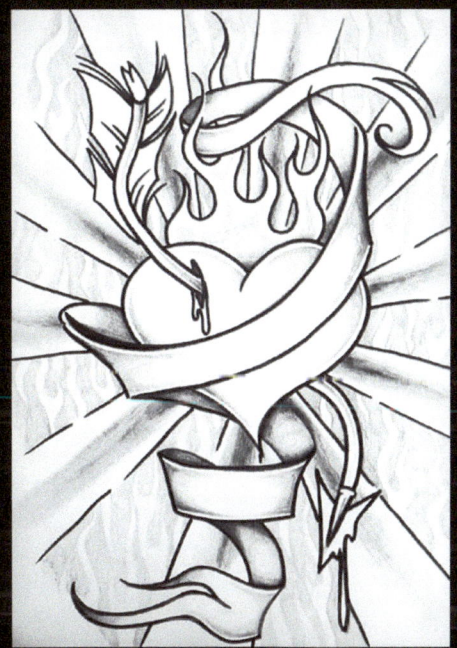

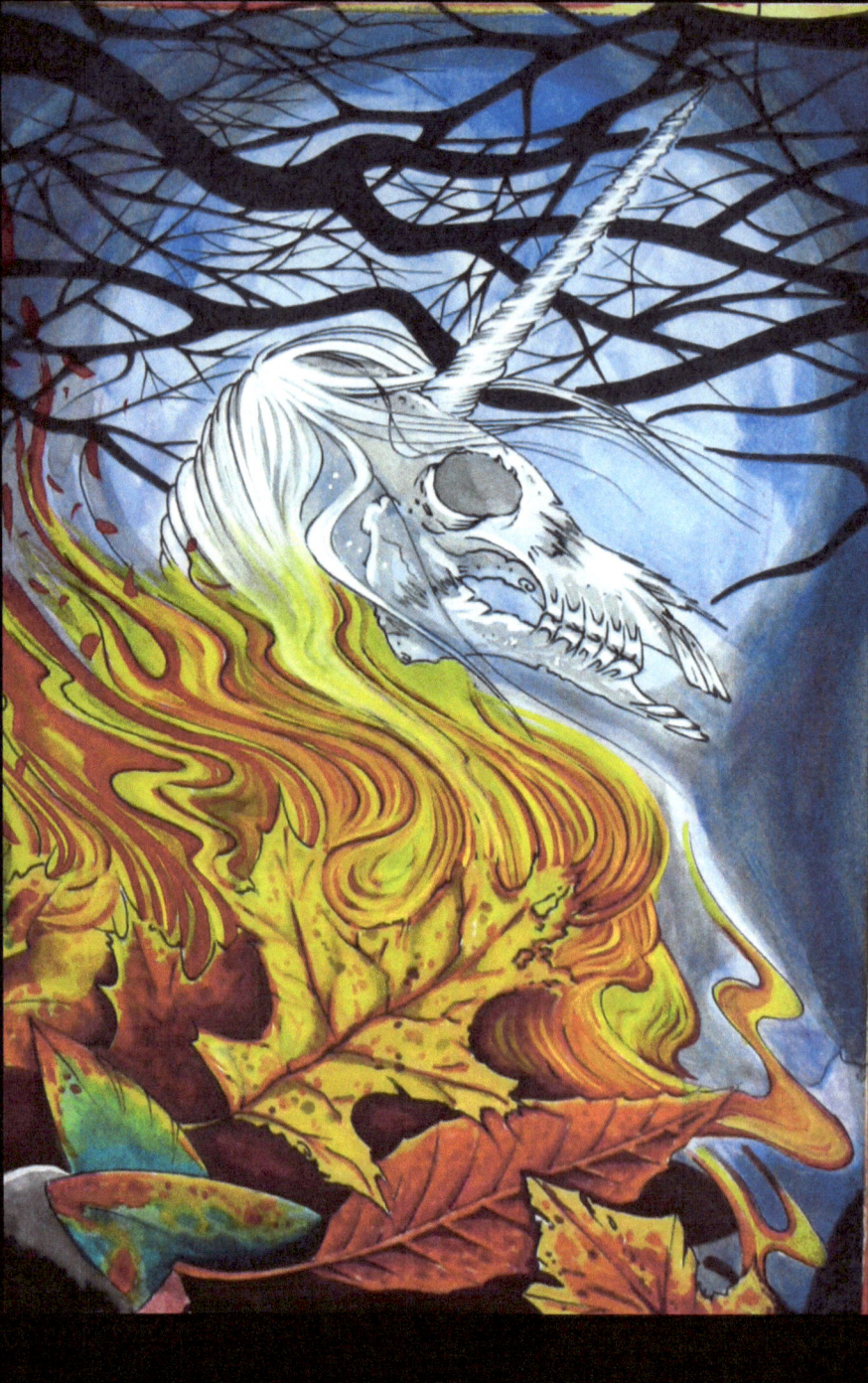

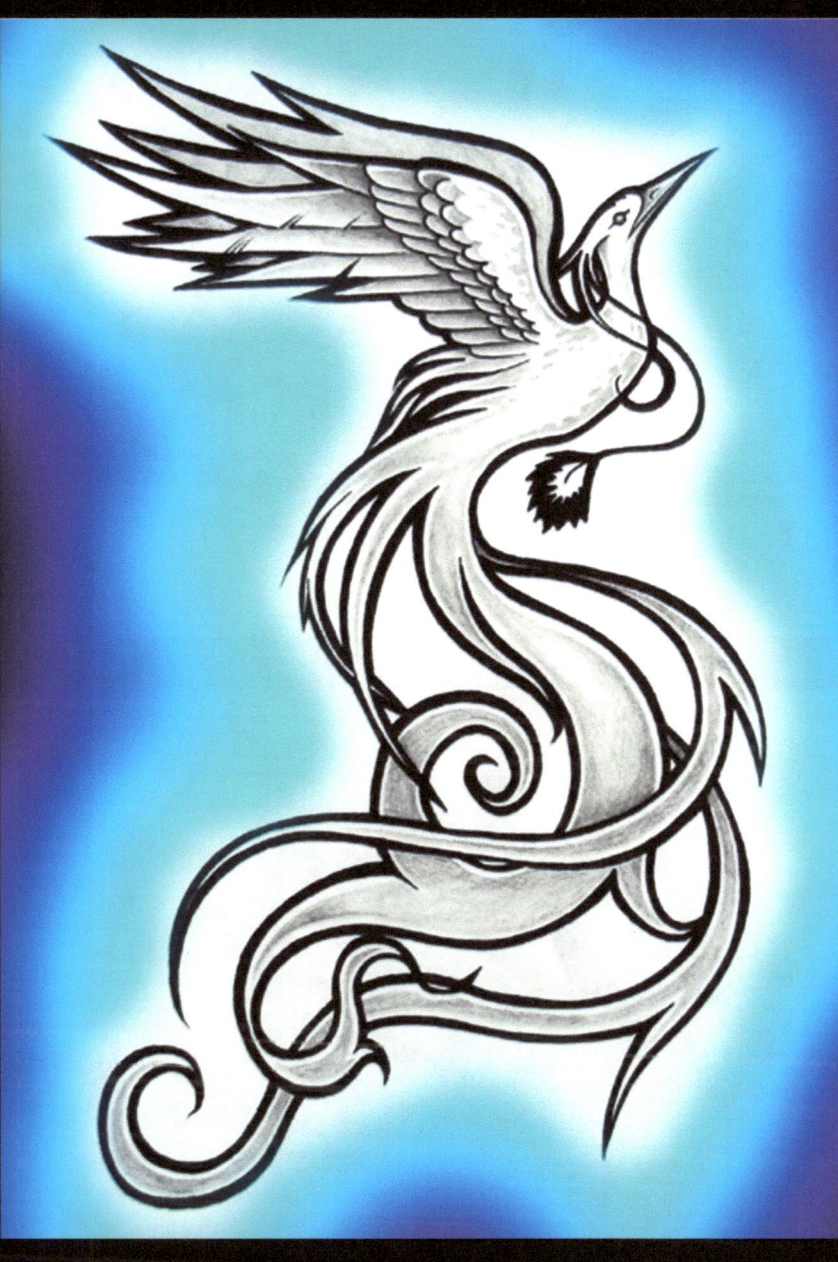

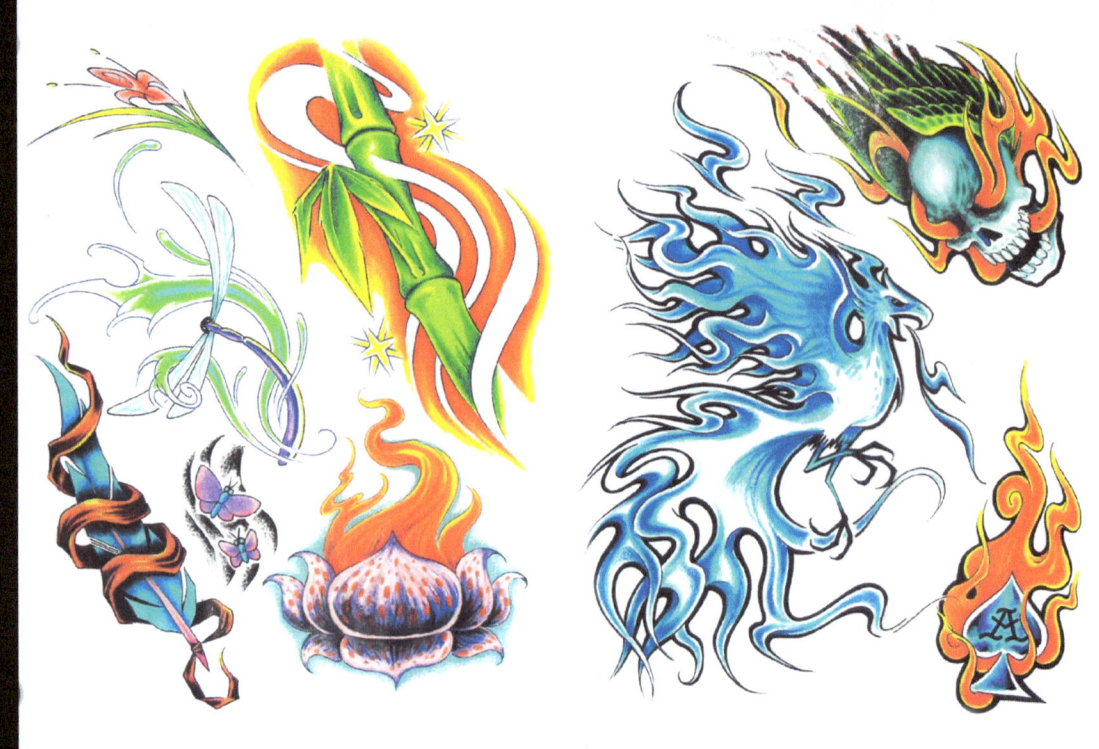

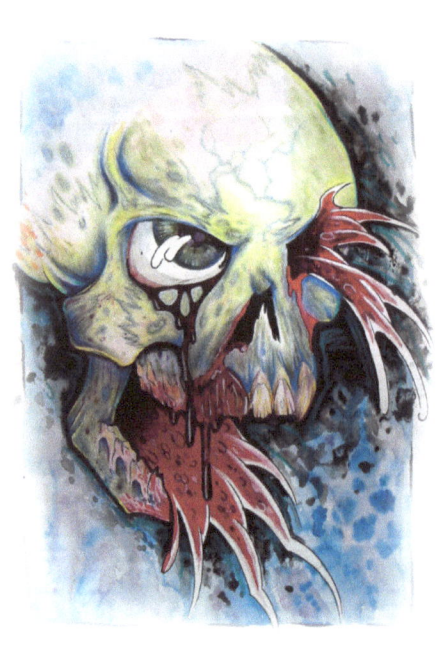

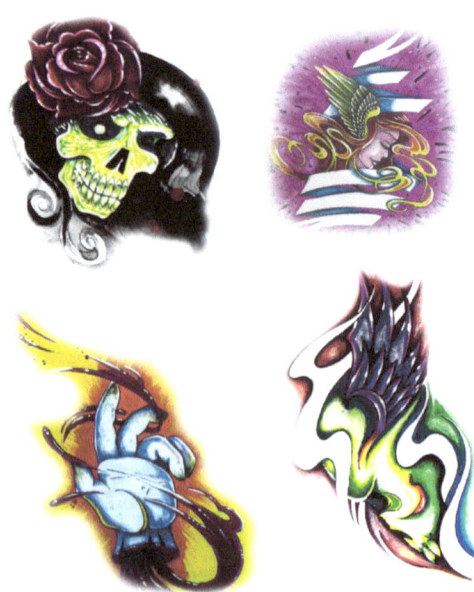

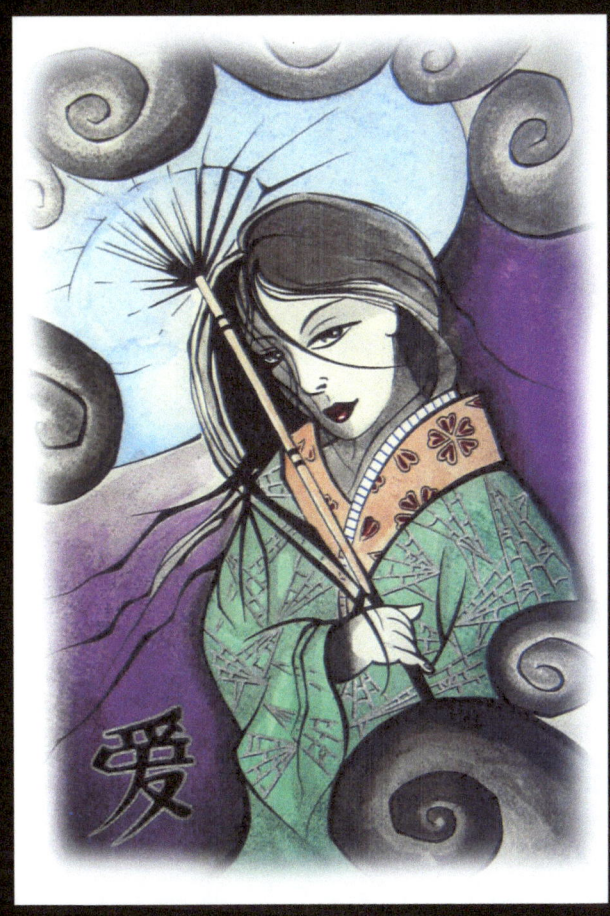

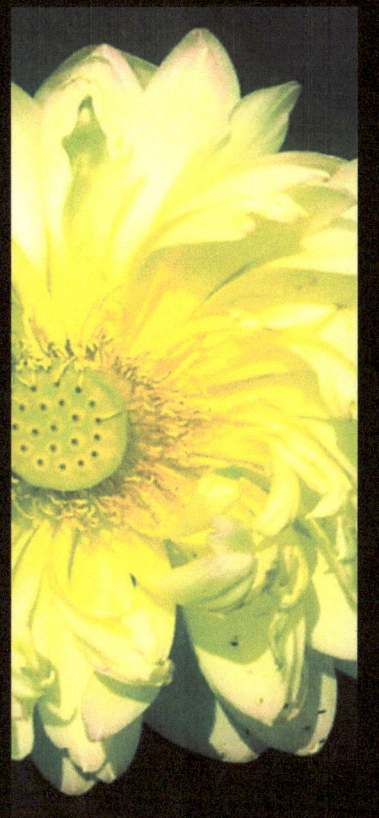

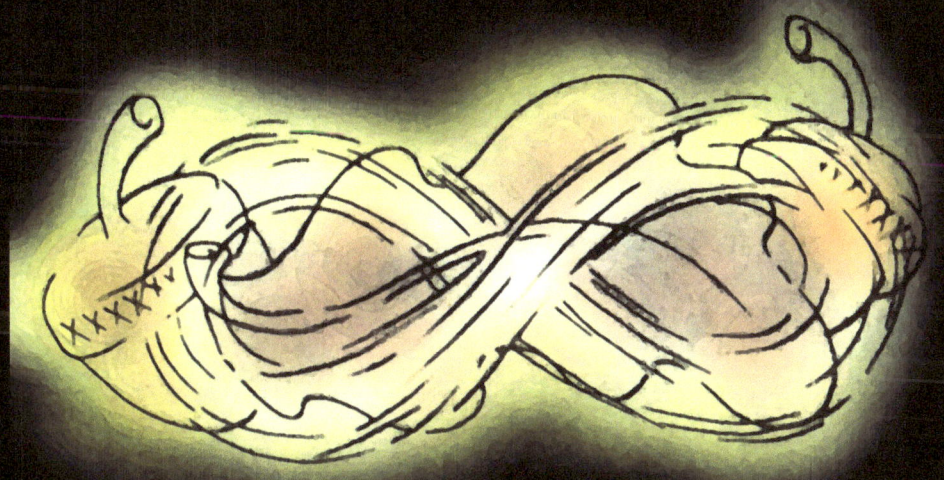

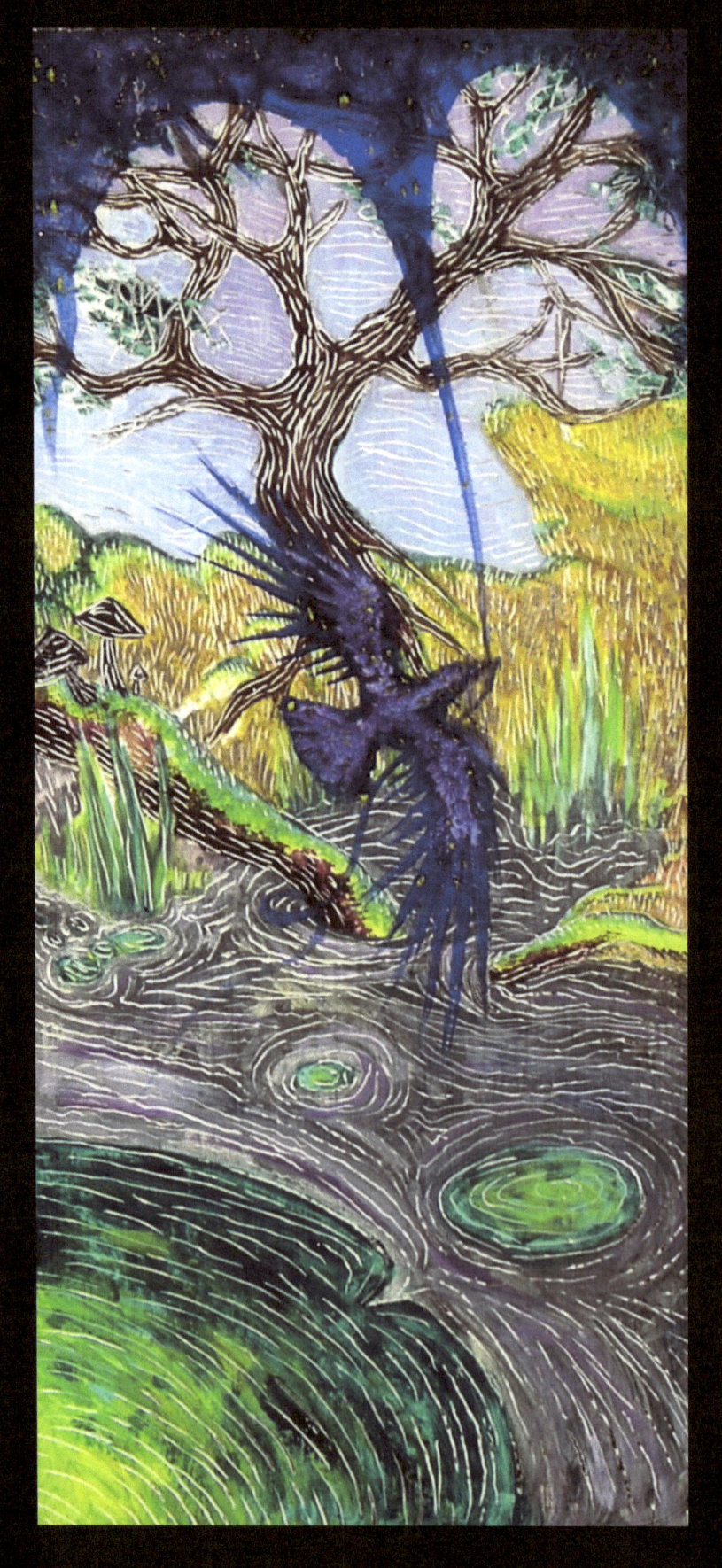

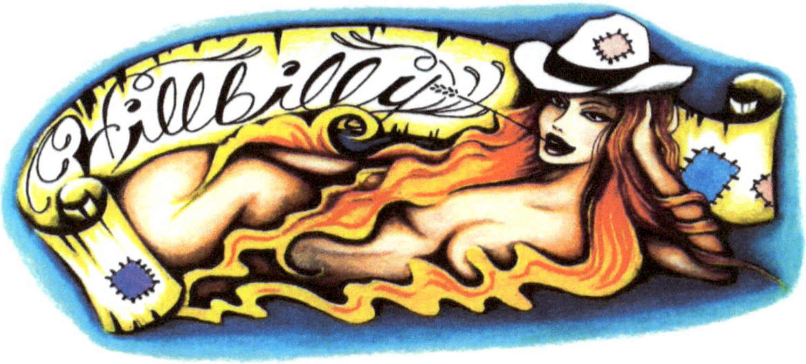

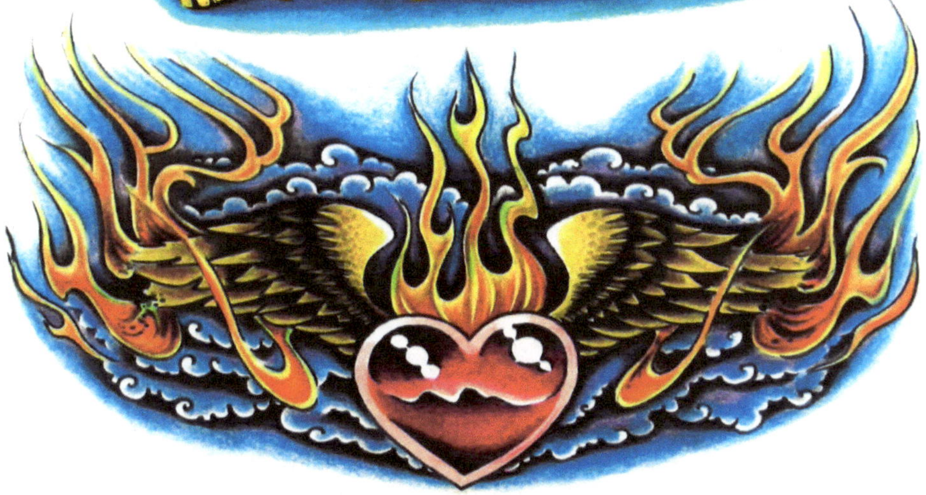

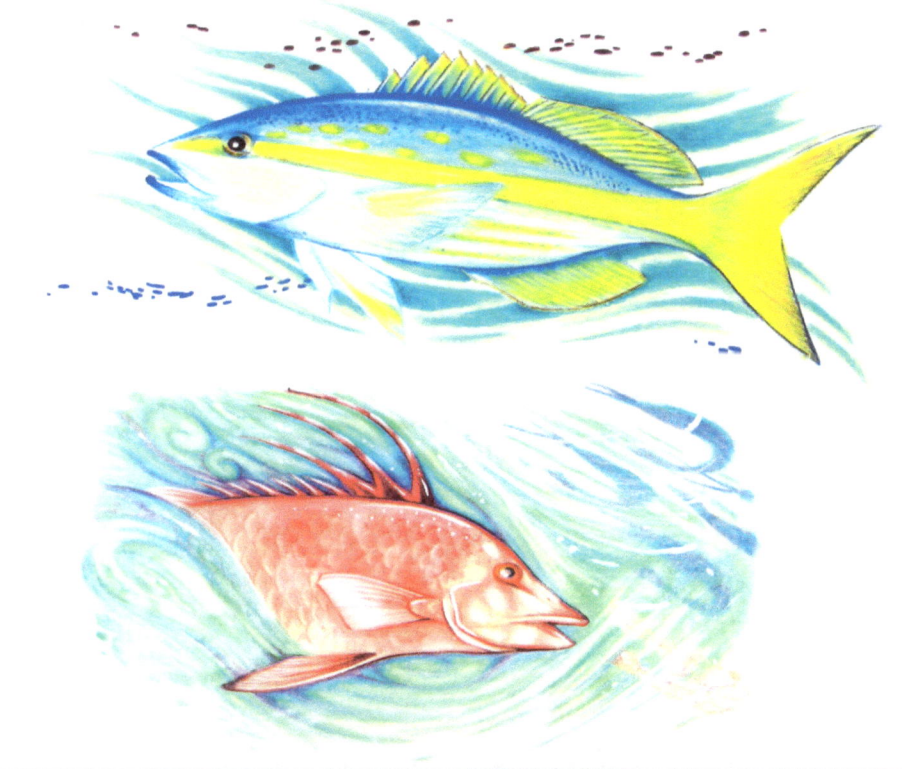

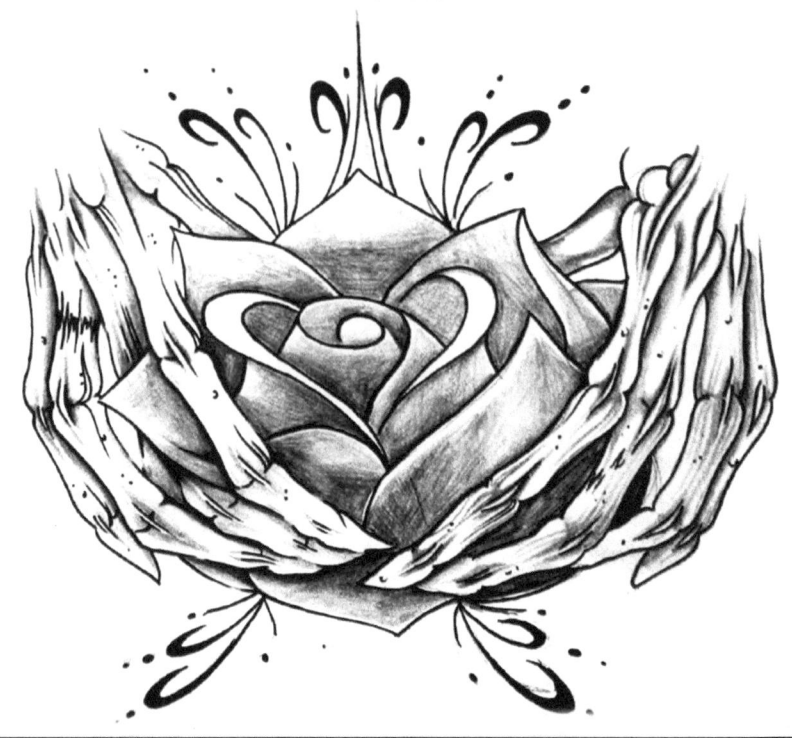
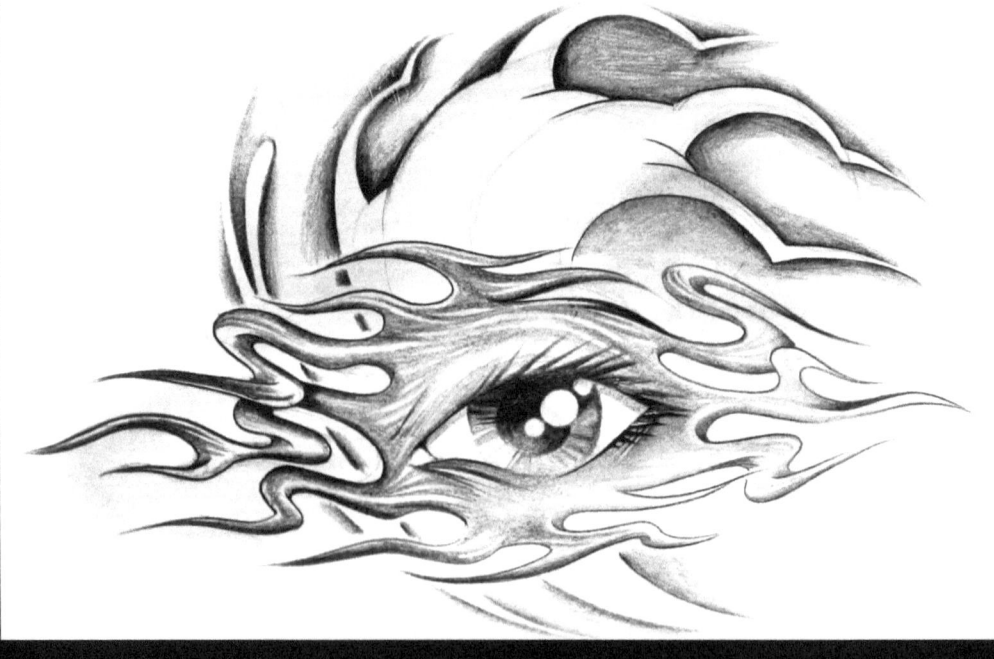

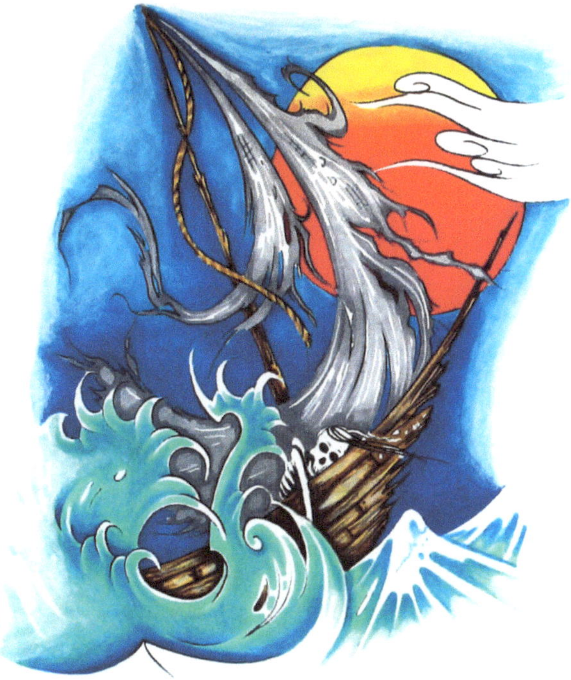

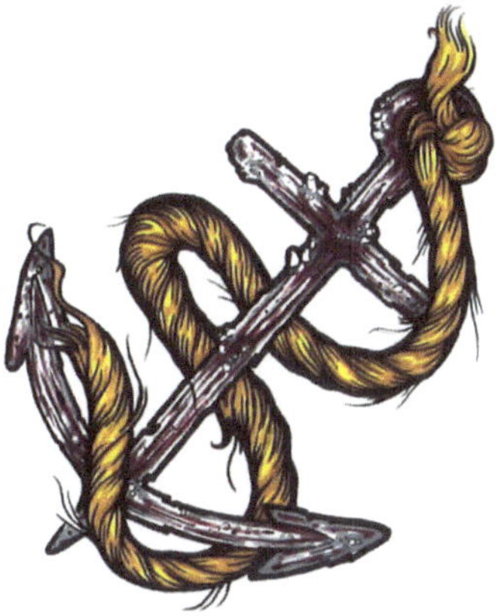

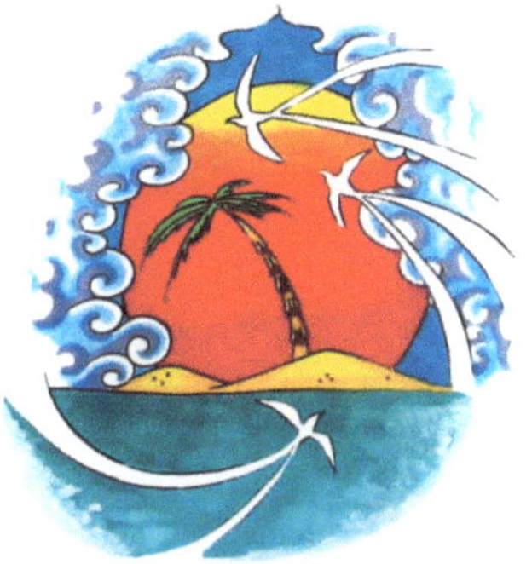

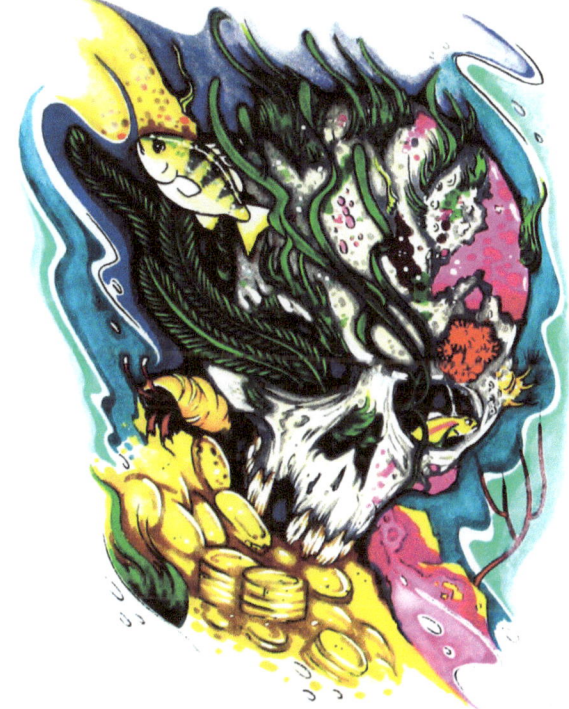
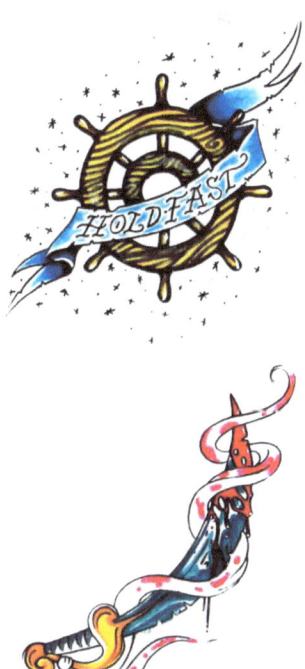

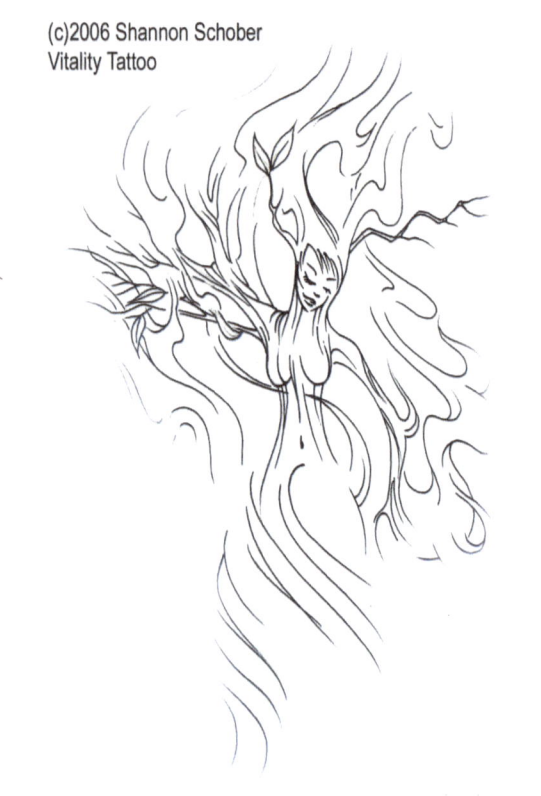

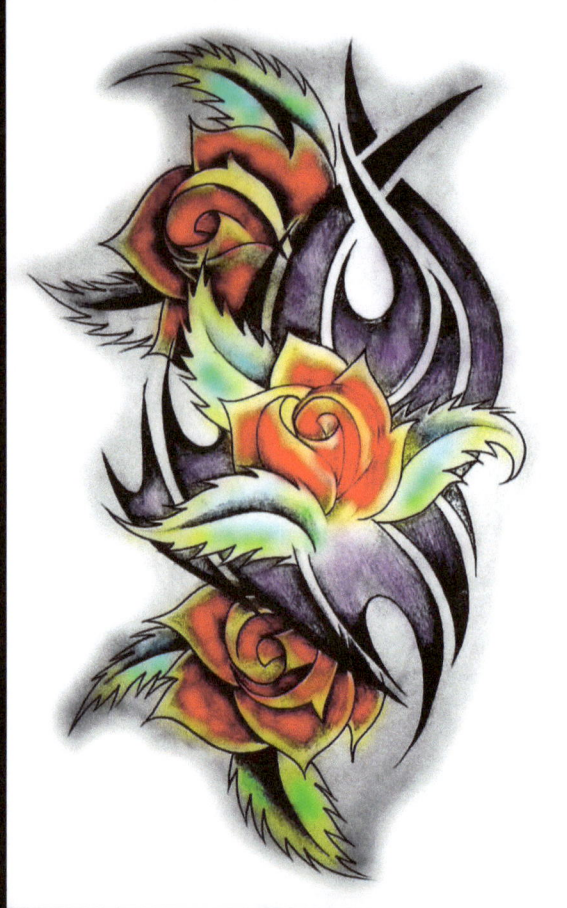

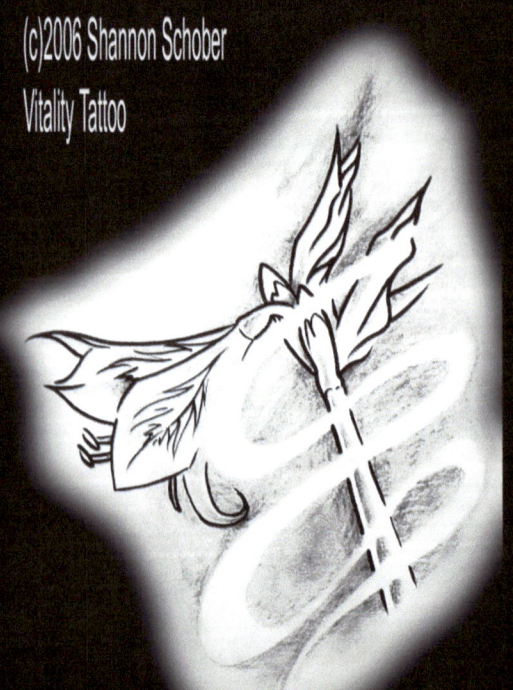

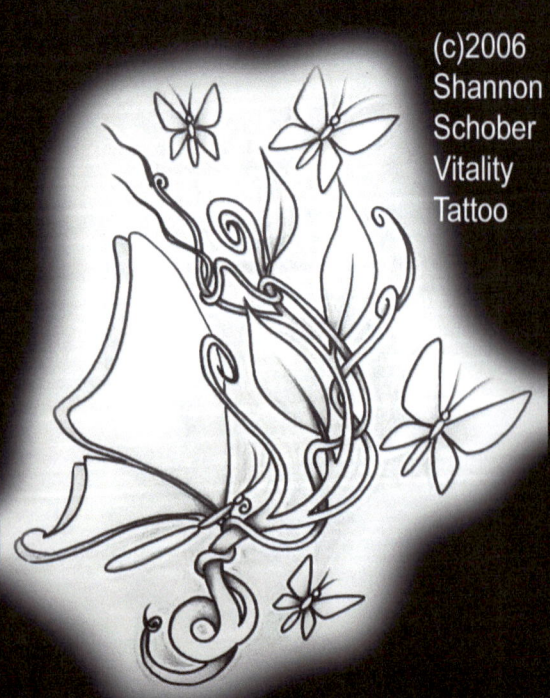

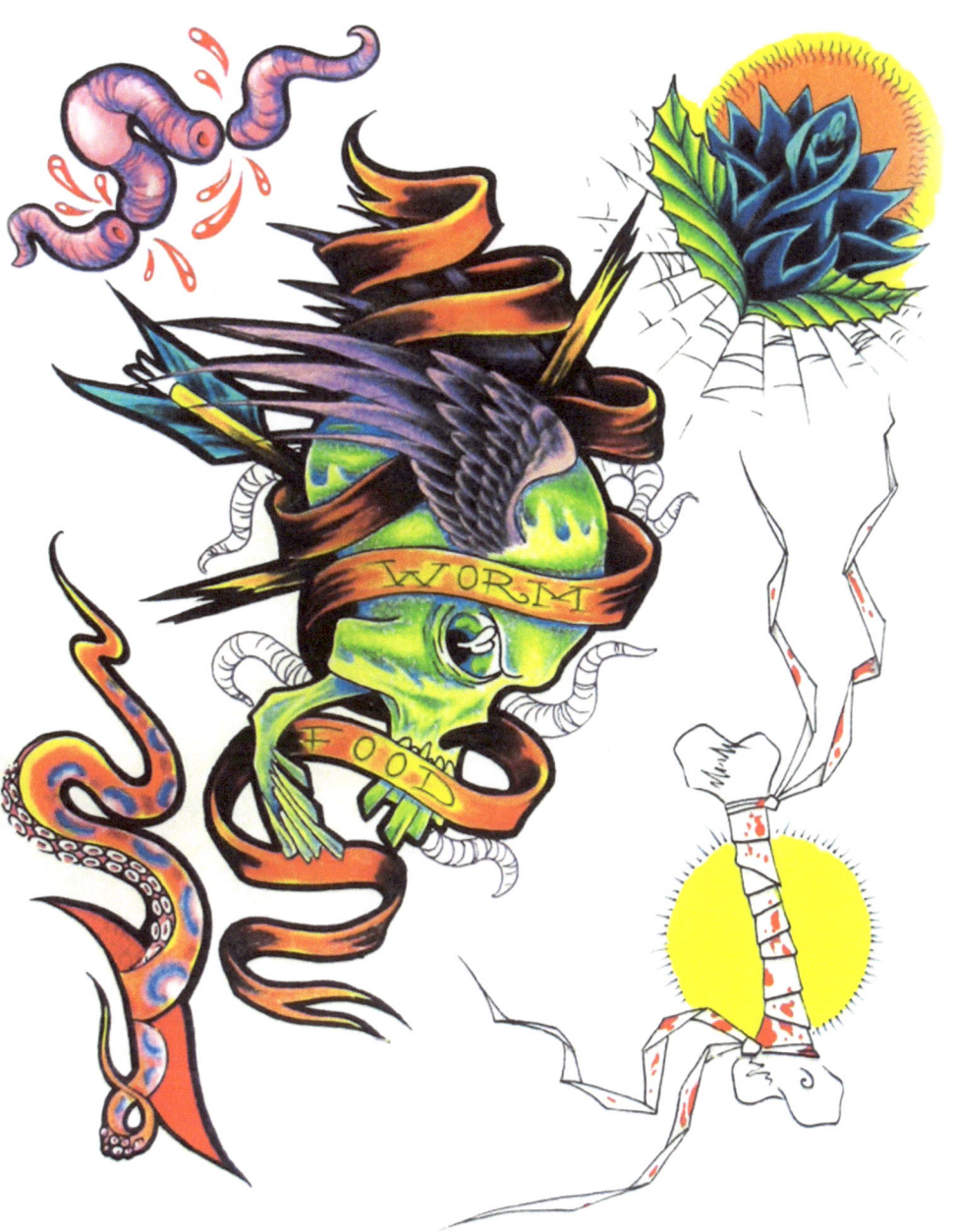

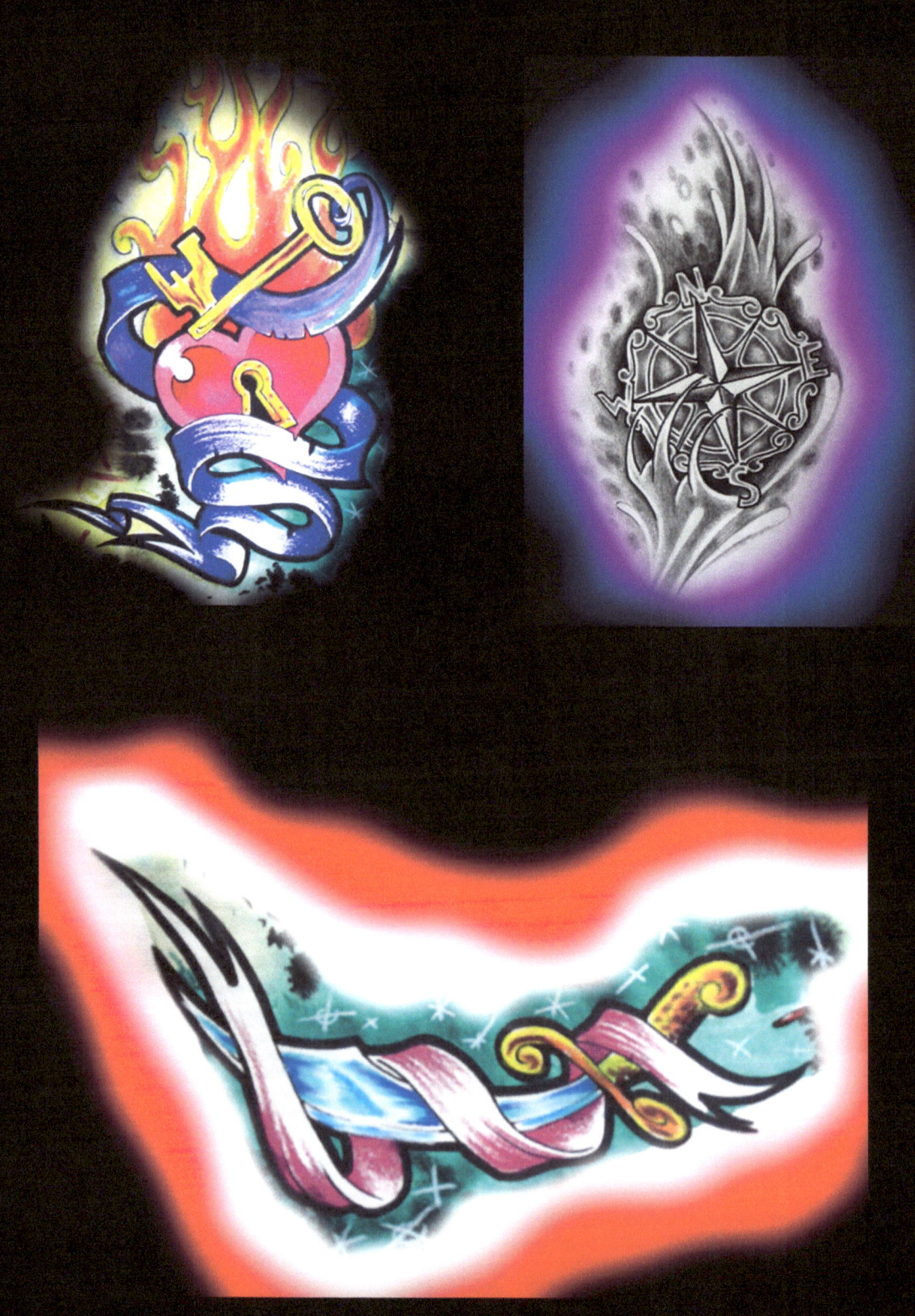

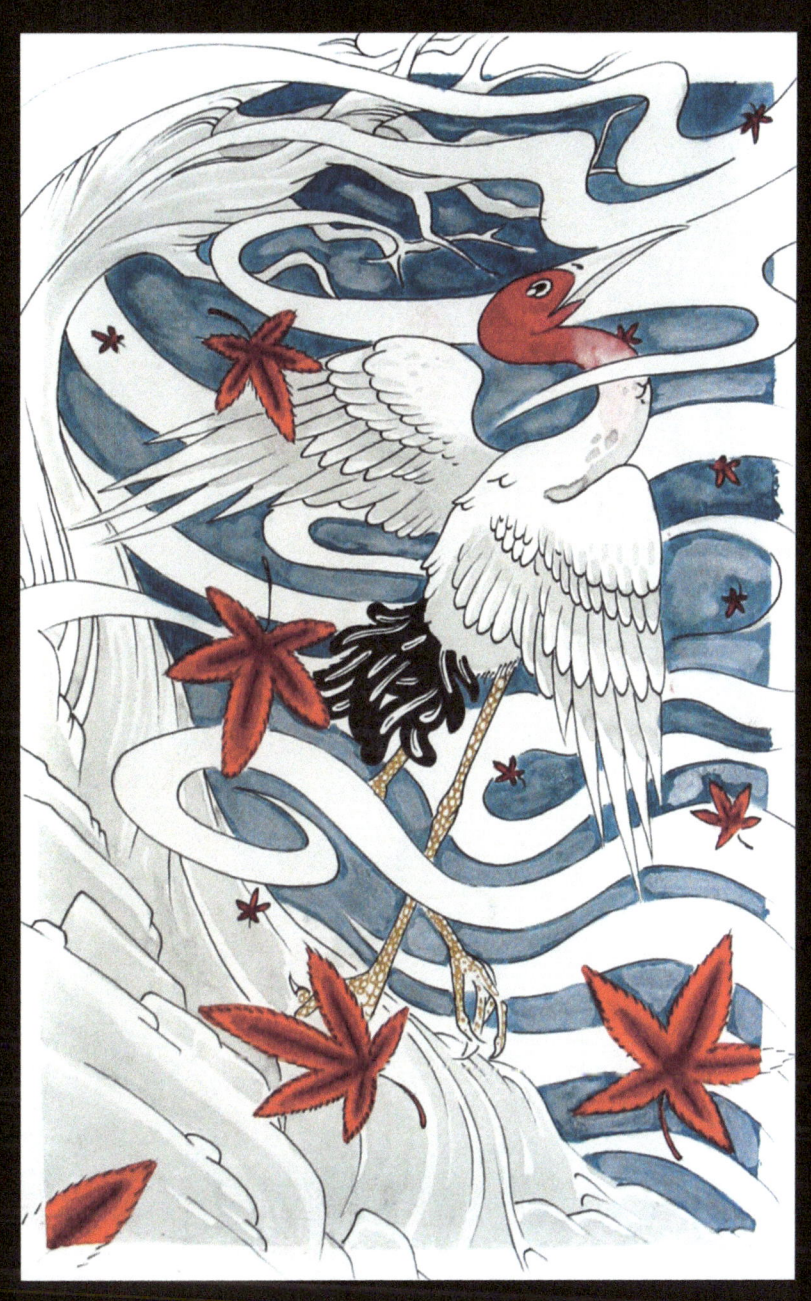

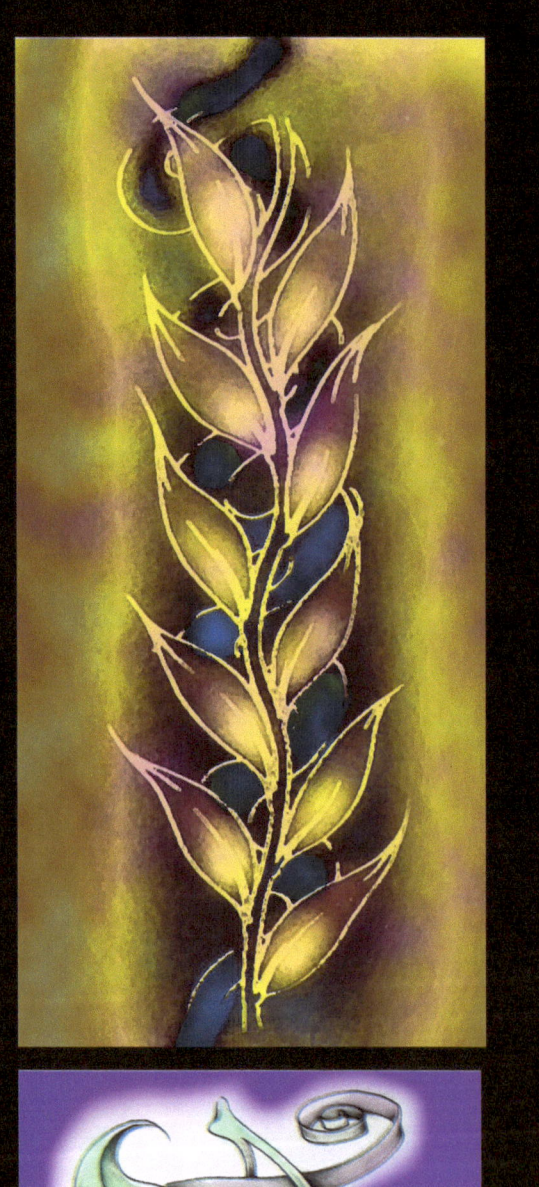

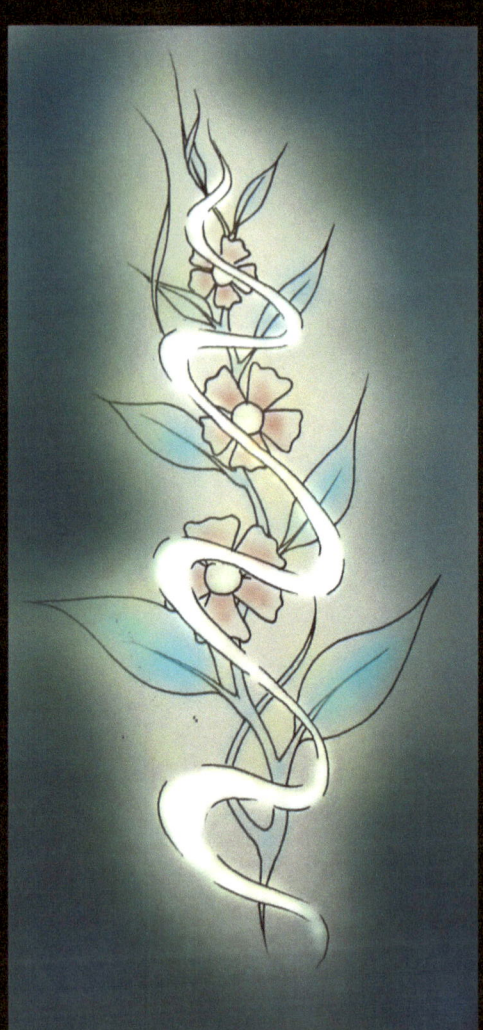

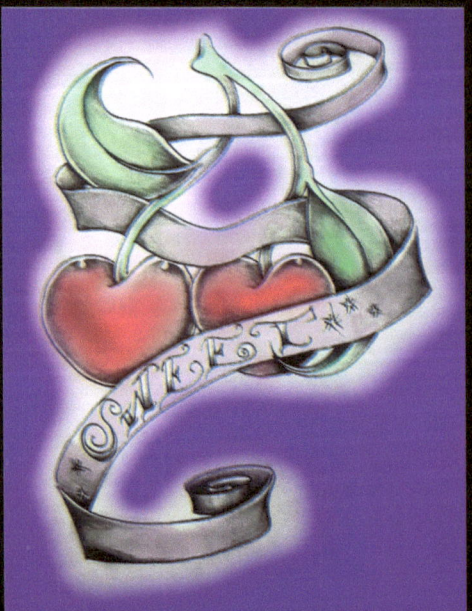

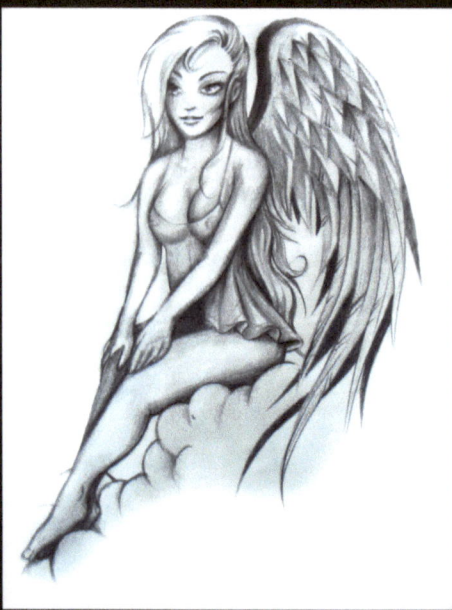

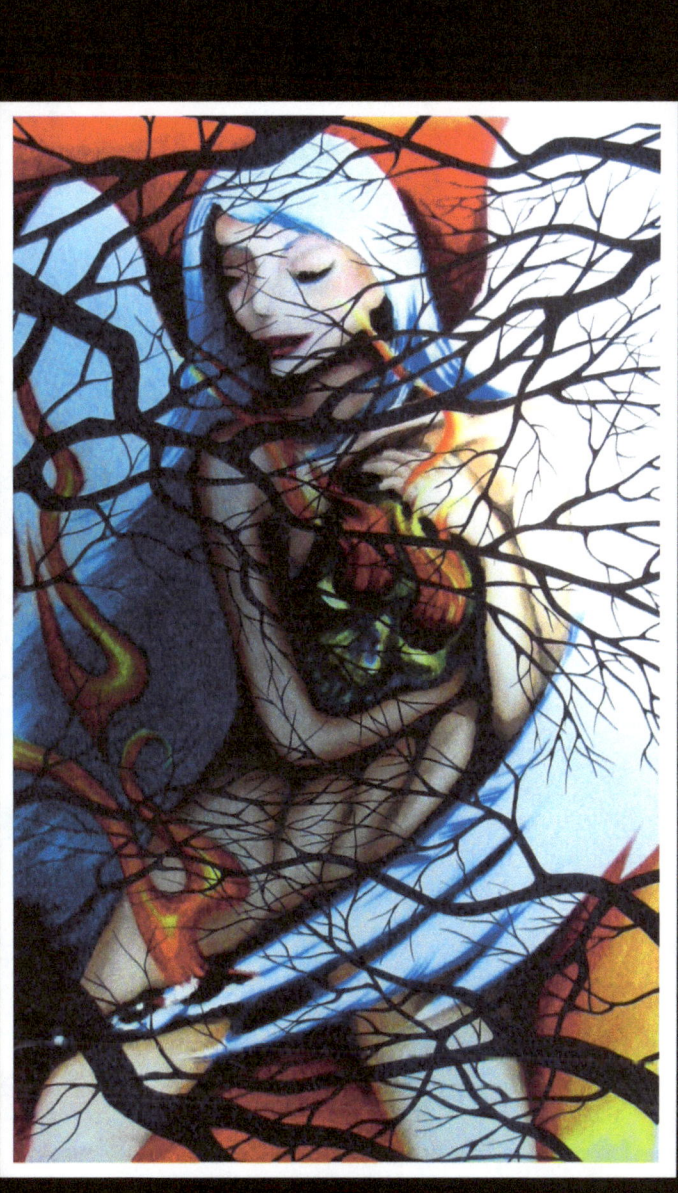

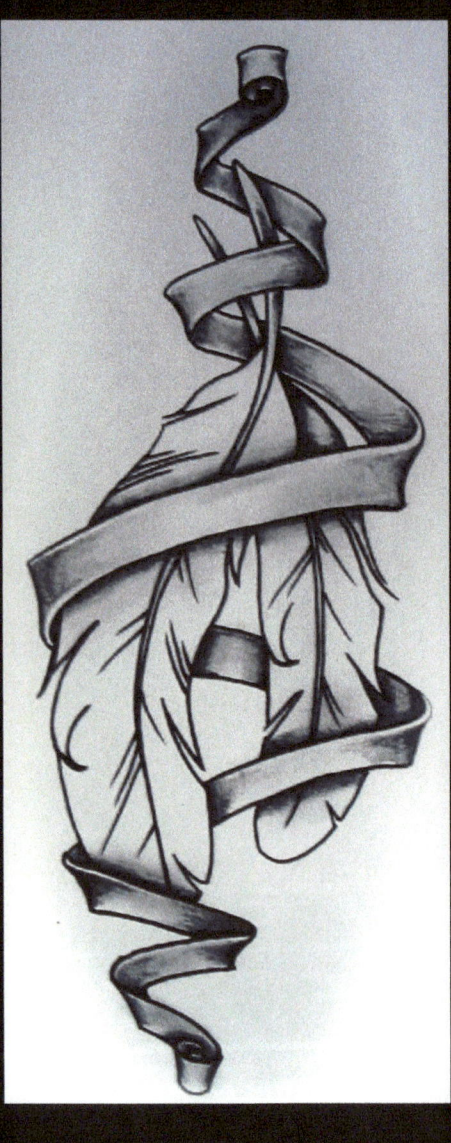

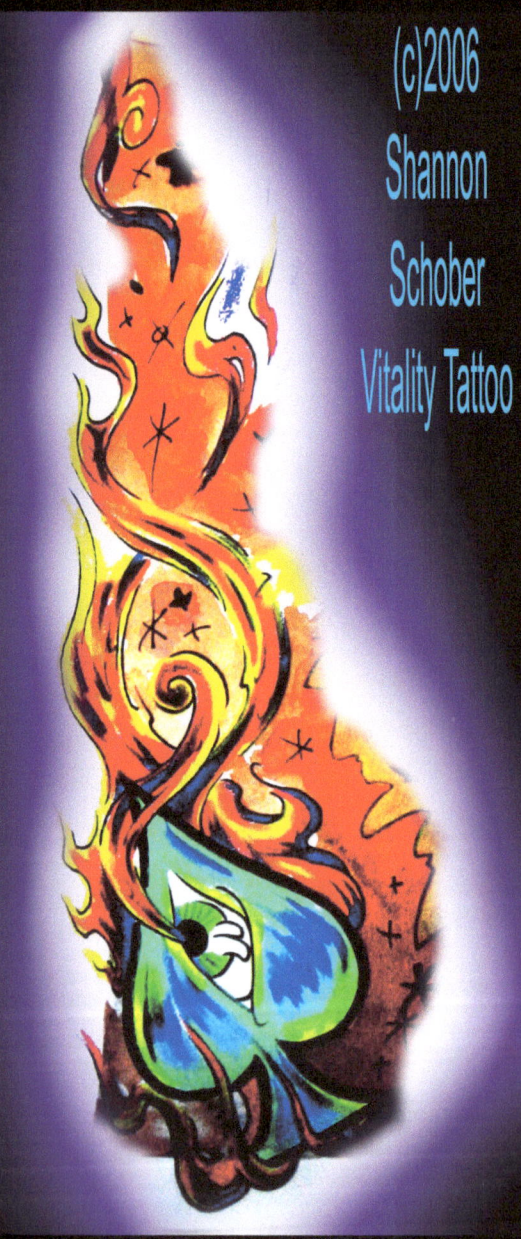

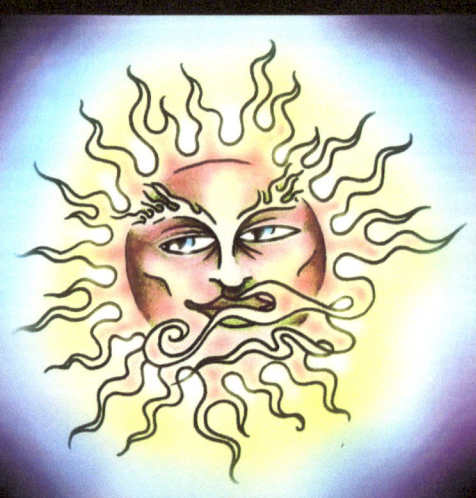

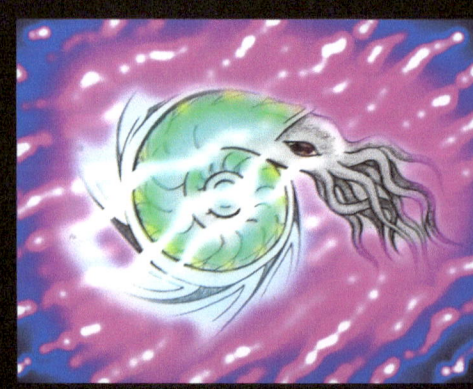

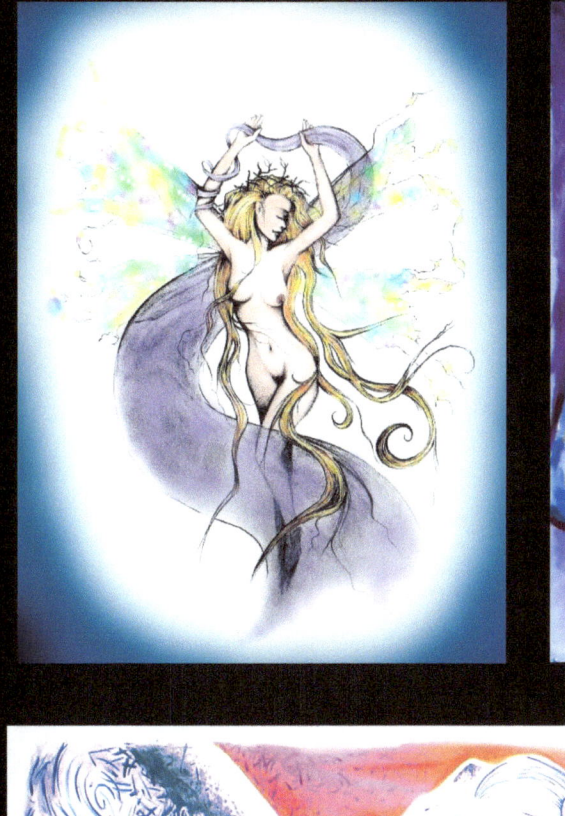
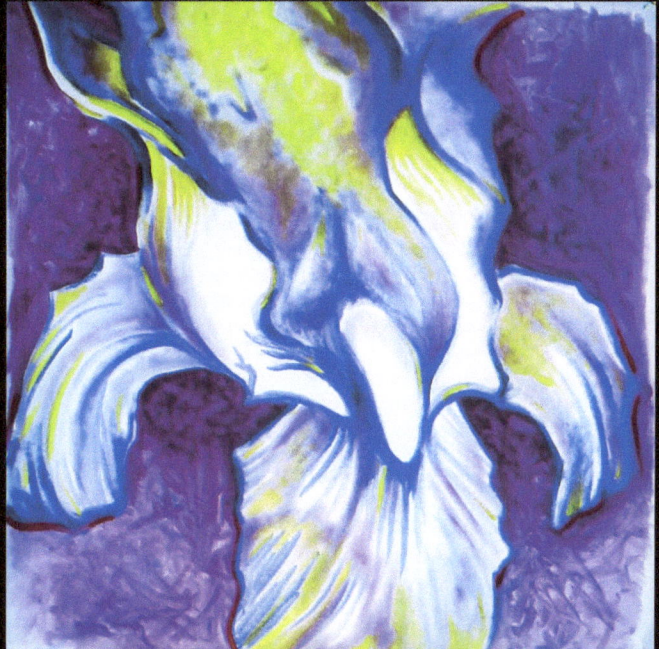
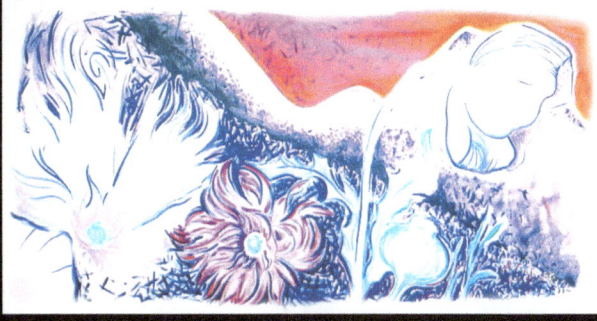
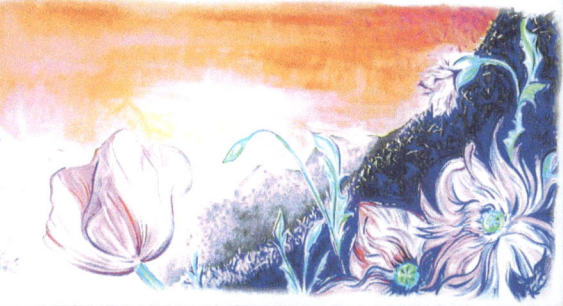
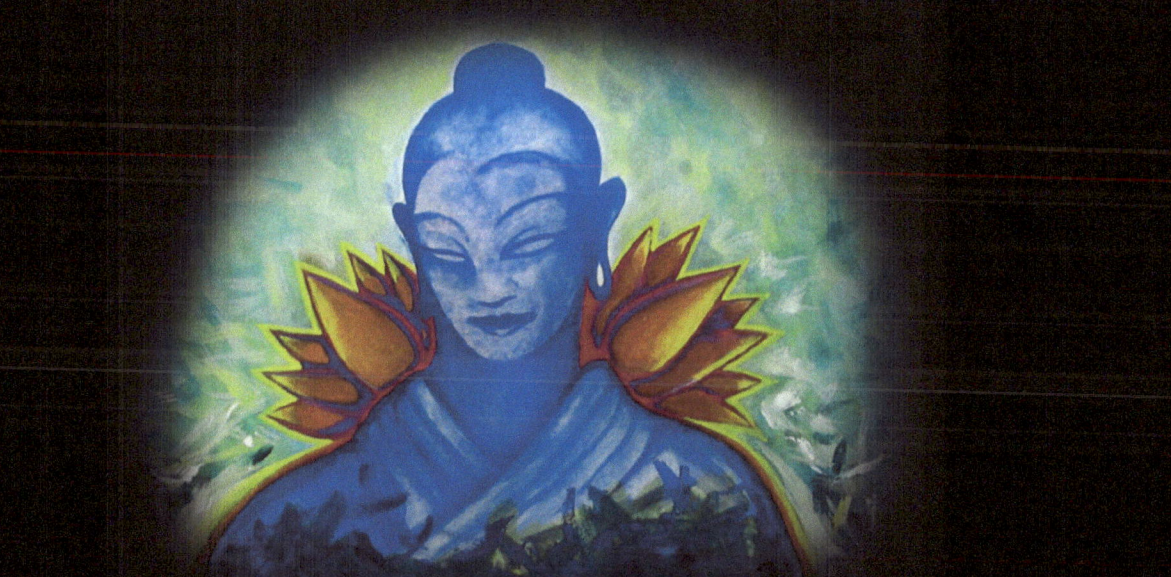

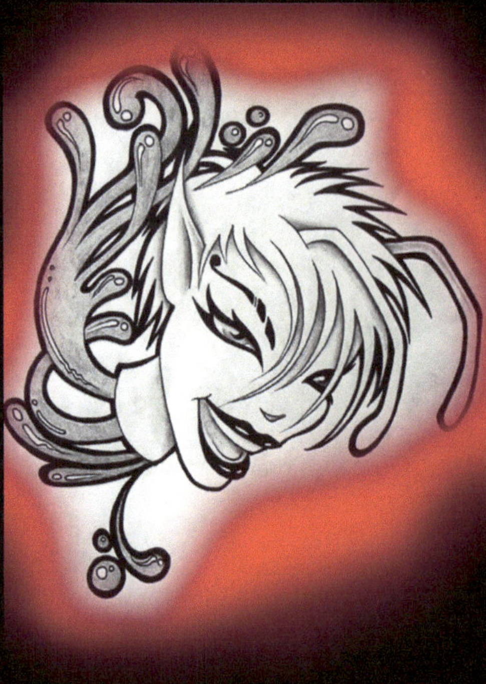

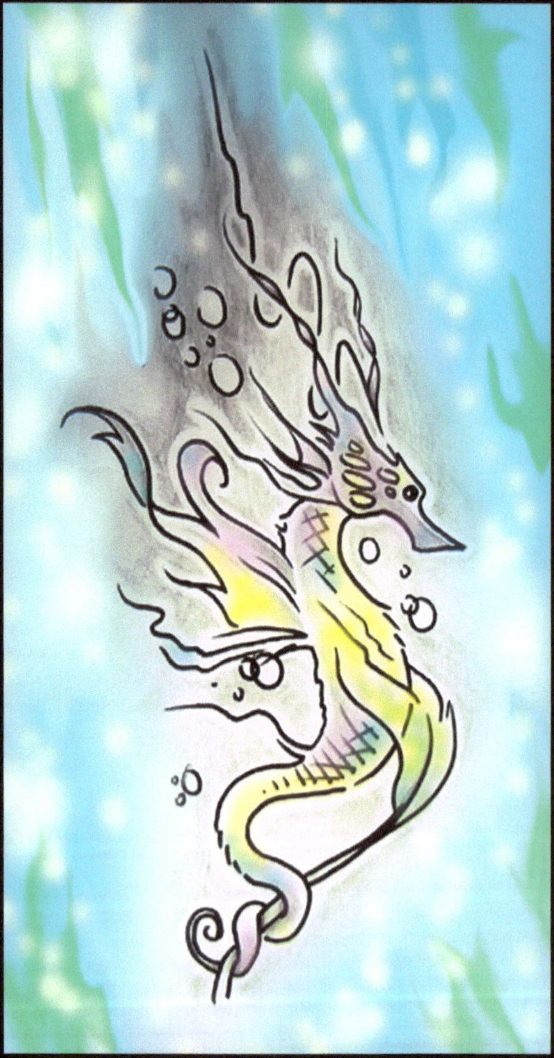

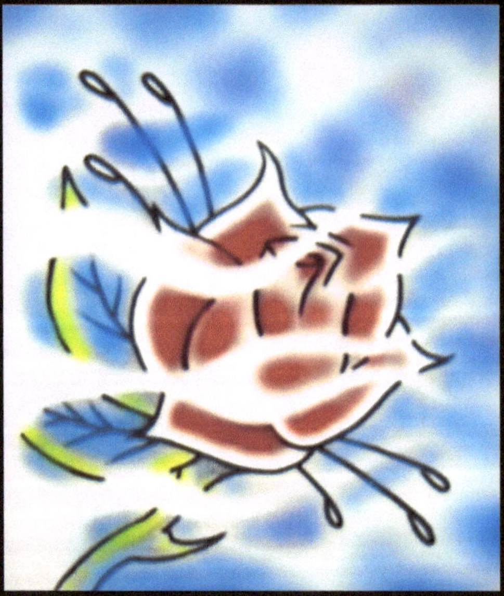

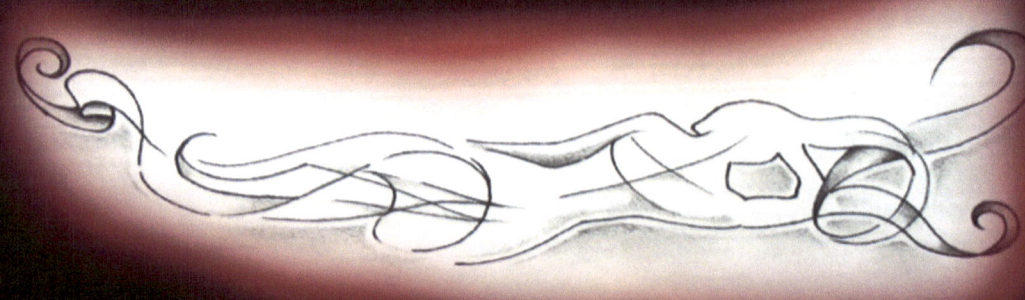

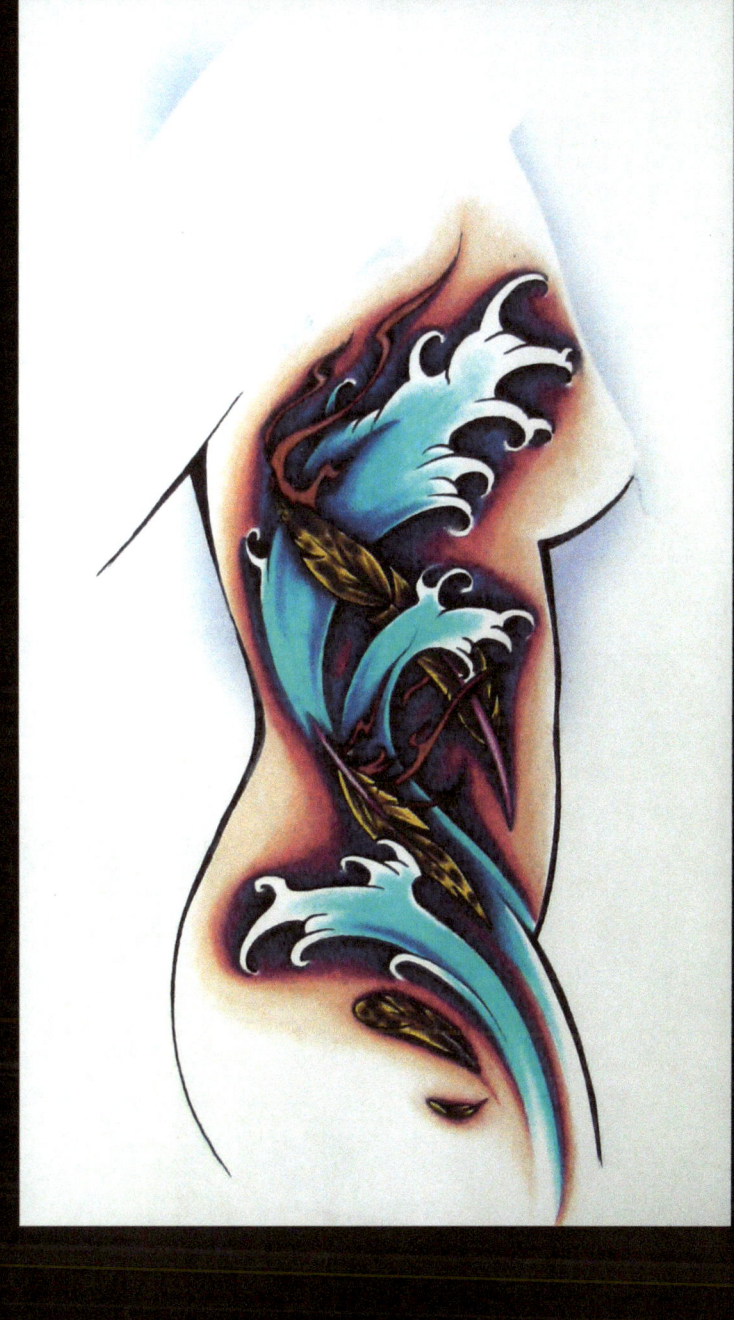

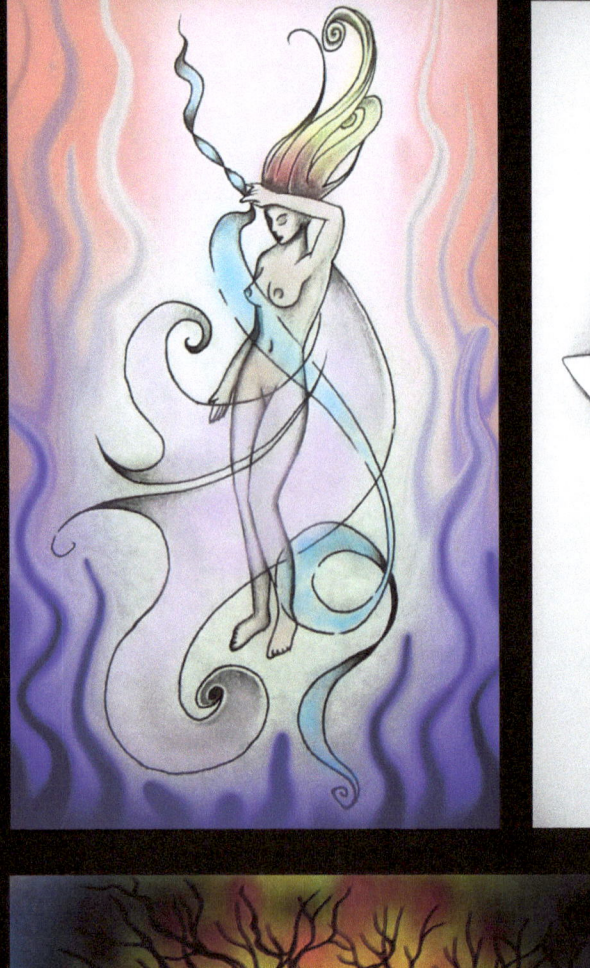
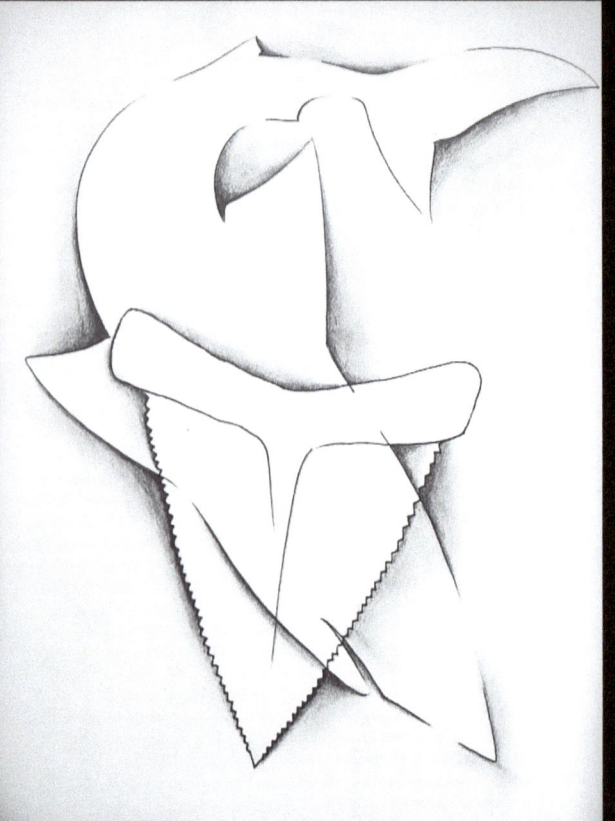
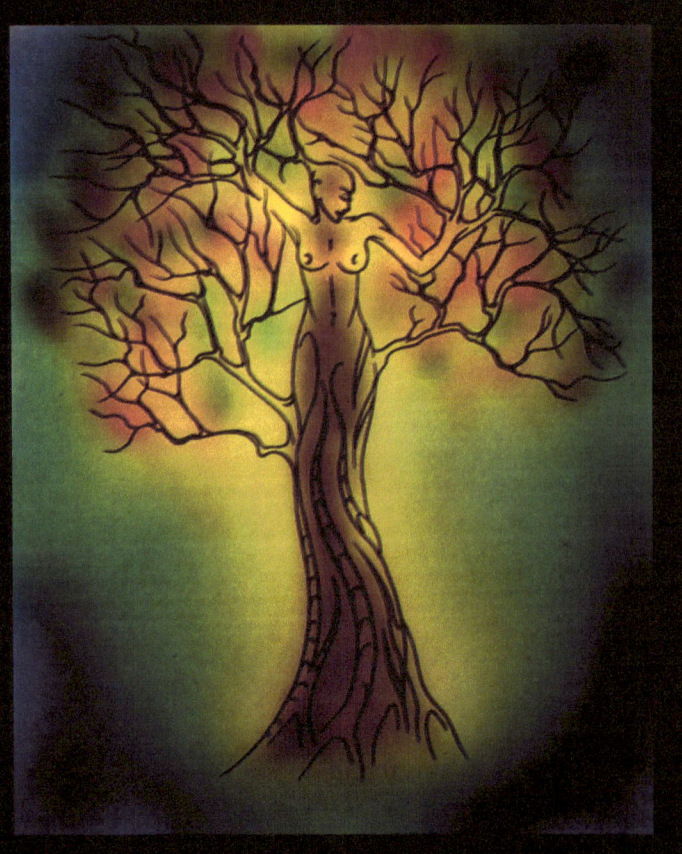
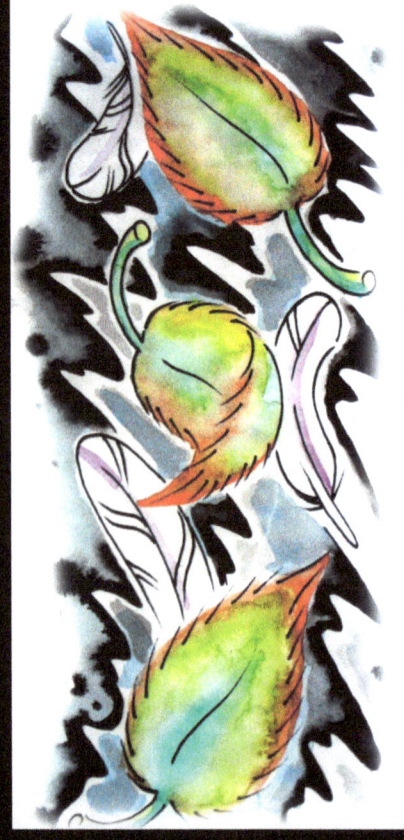

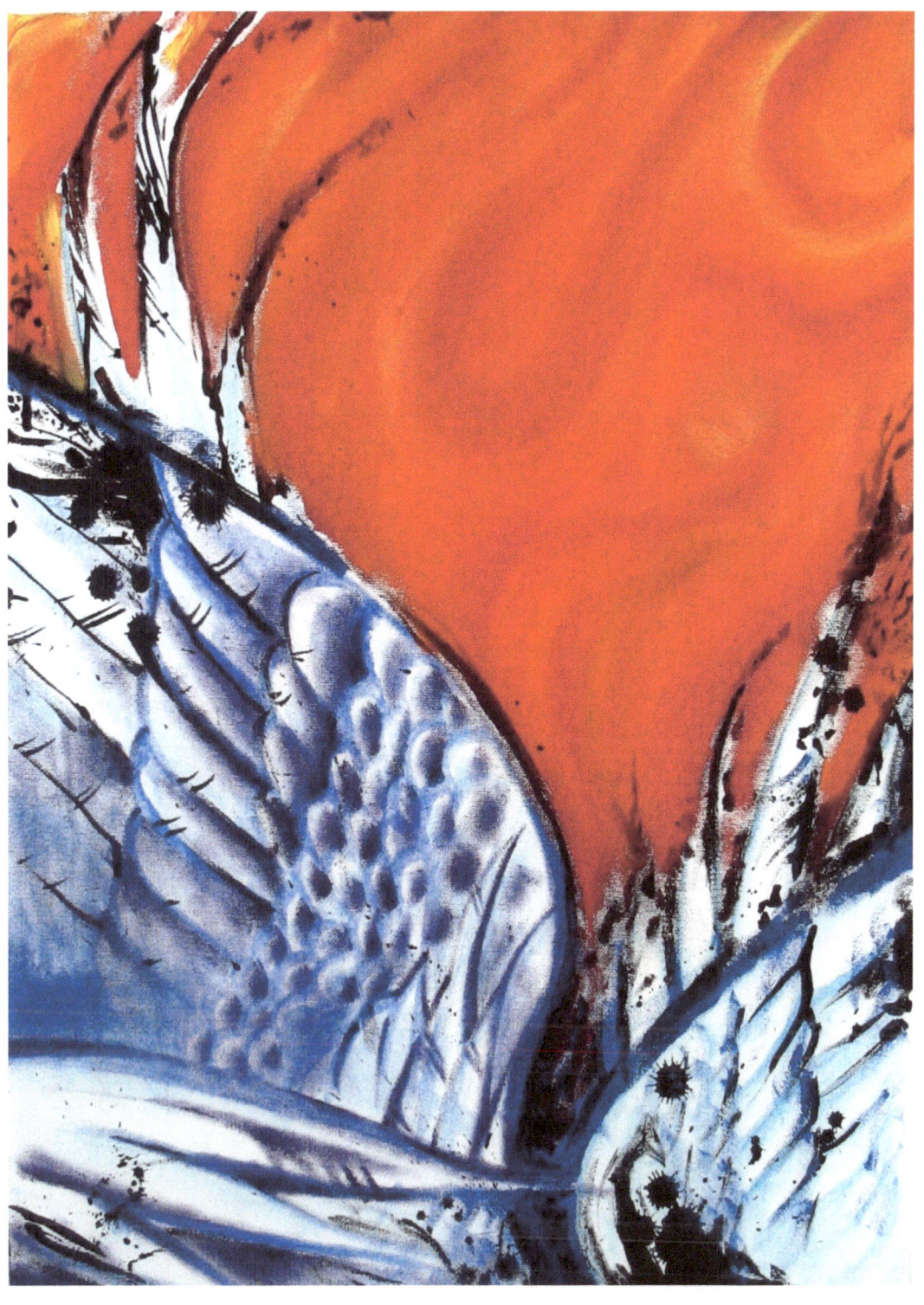

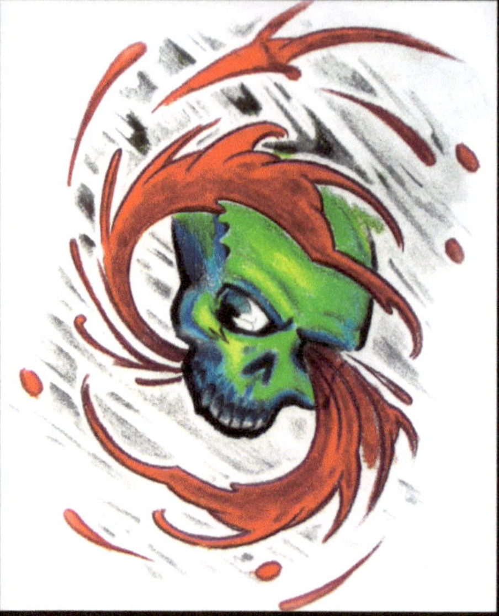

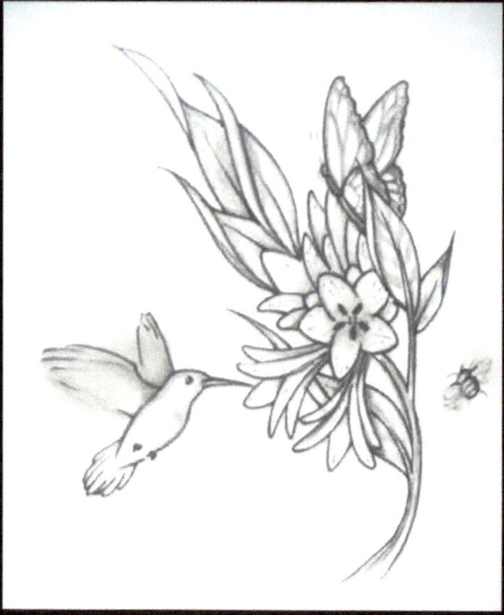

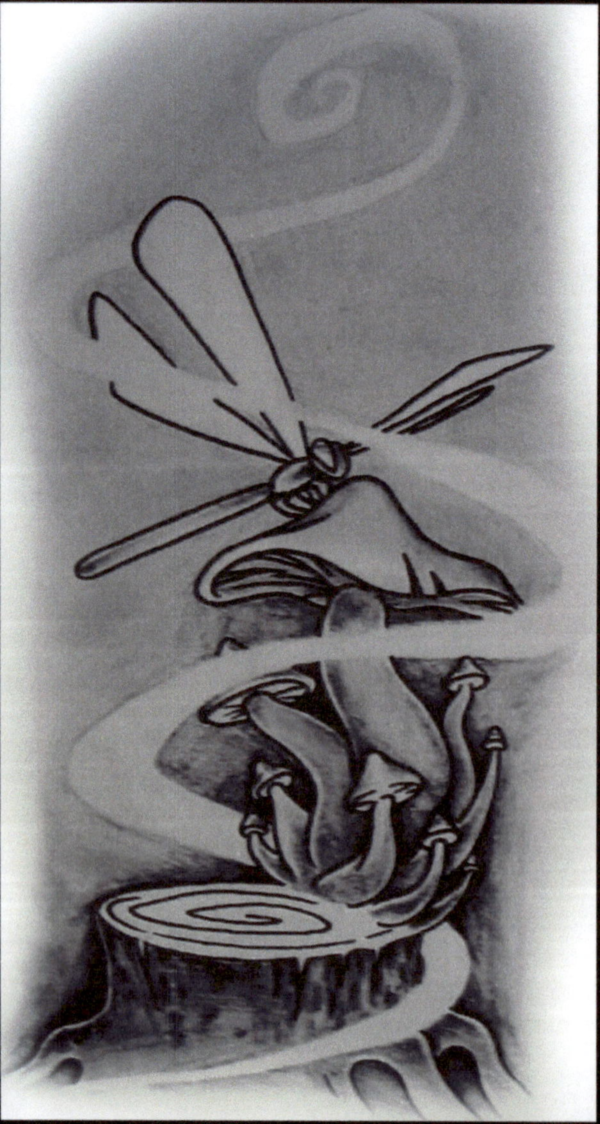

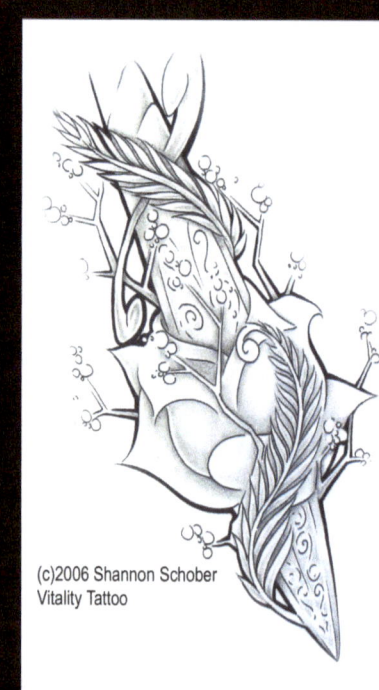

(c)2006 Shannon Schober
Vitality Tattoo

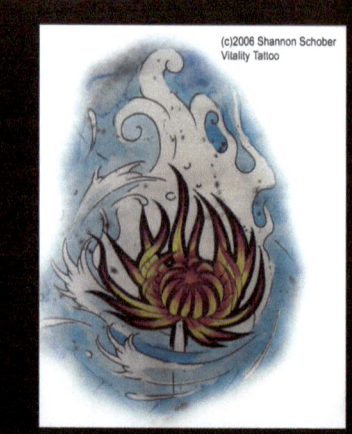

(c)2006 Shannon Schober
Vitality Tattoo

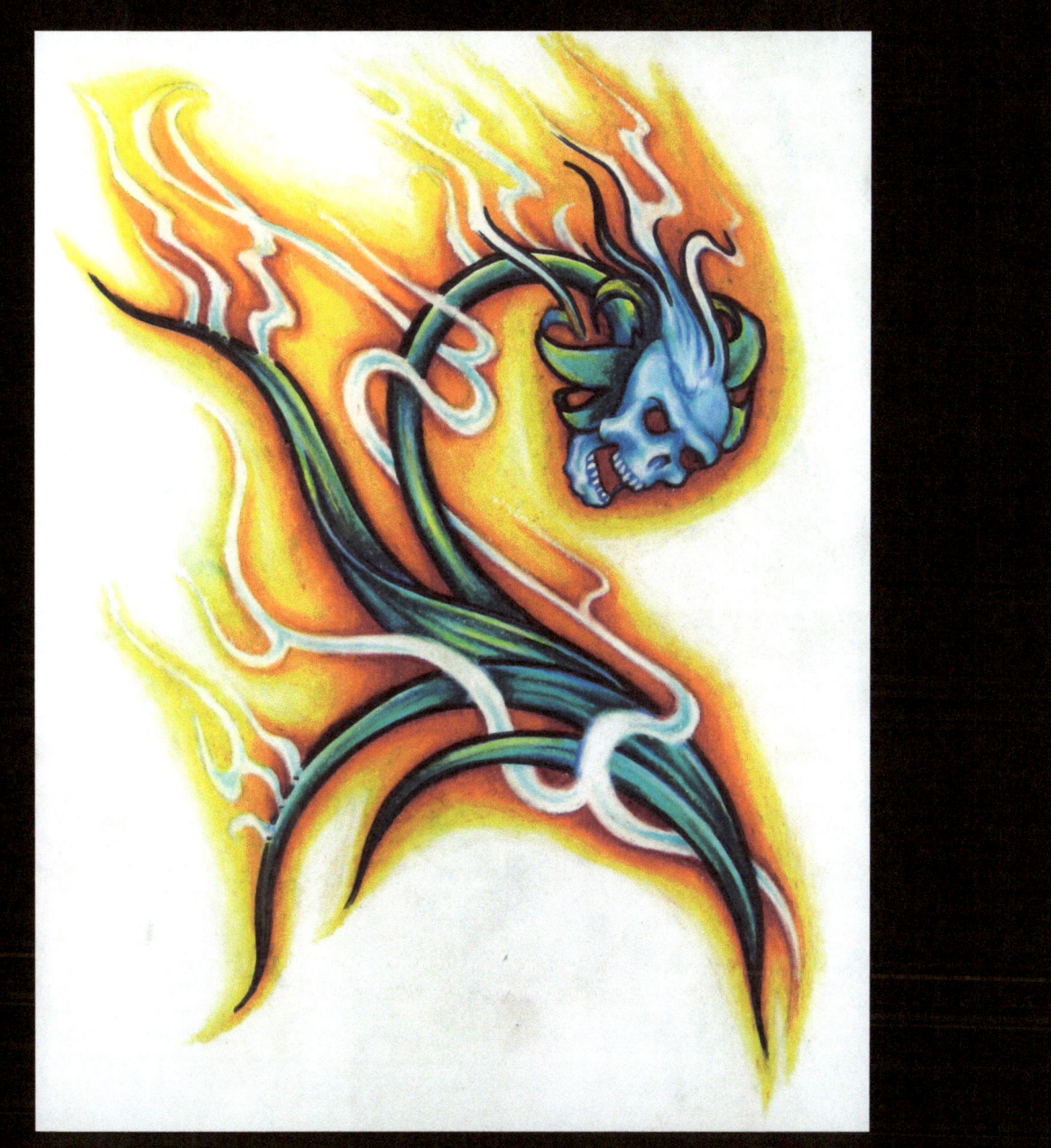

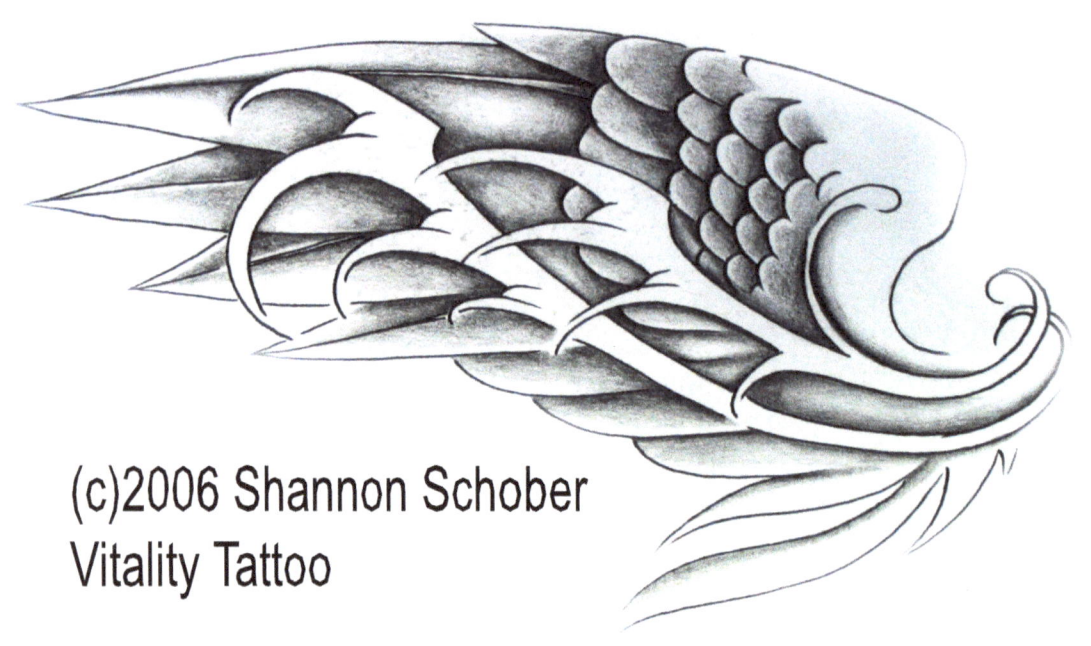

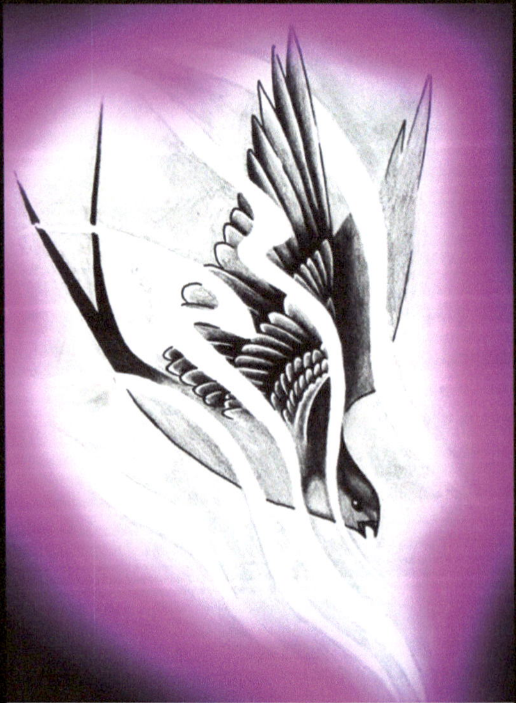

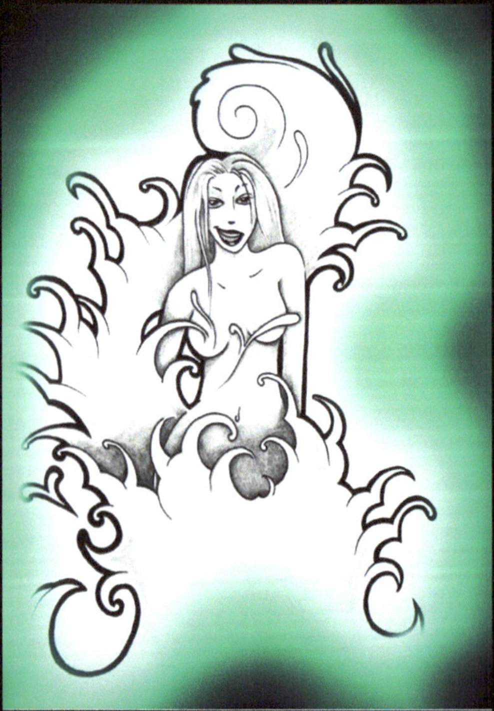

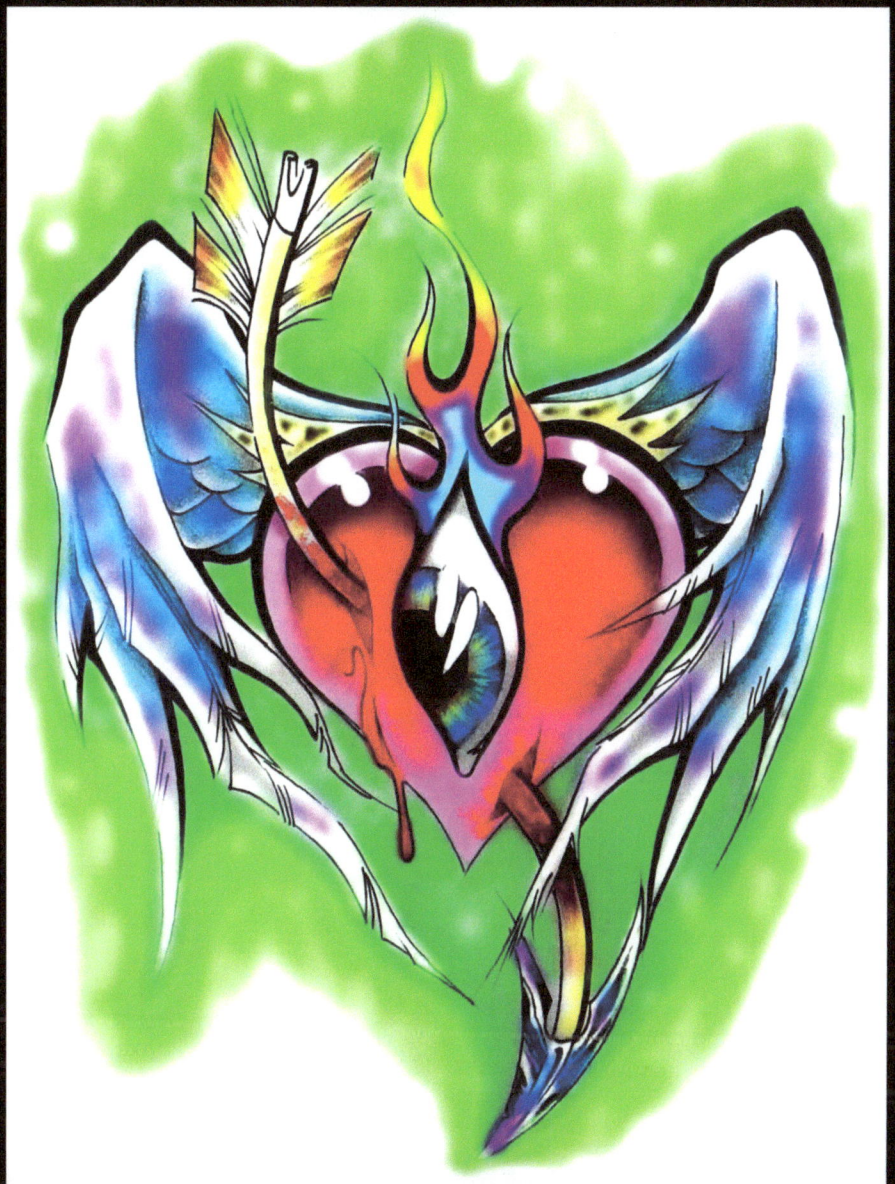

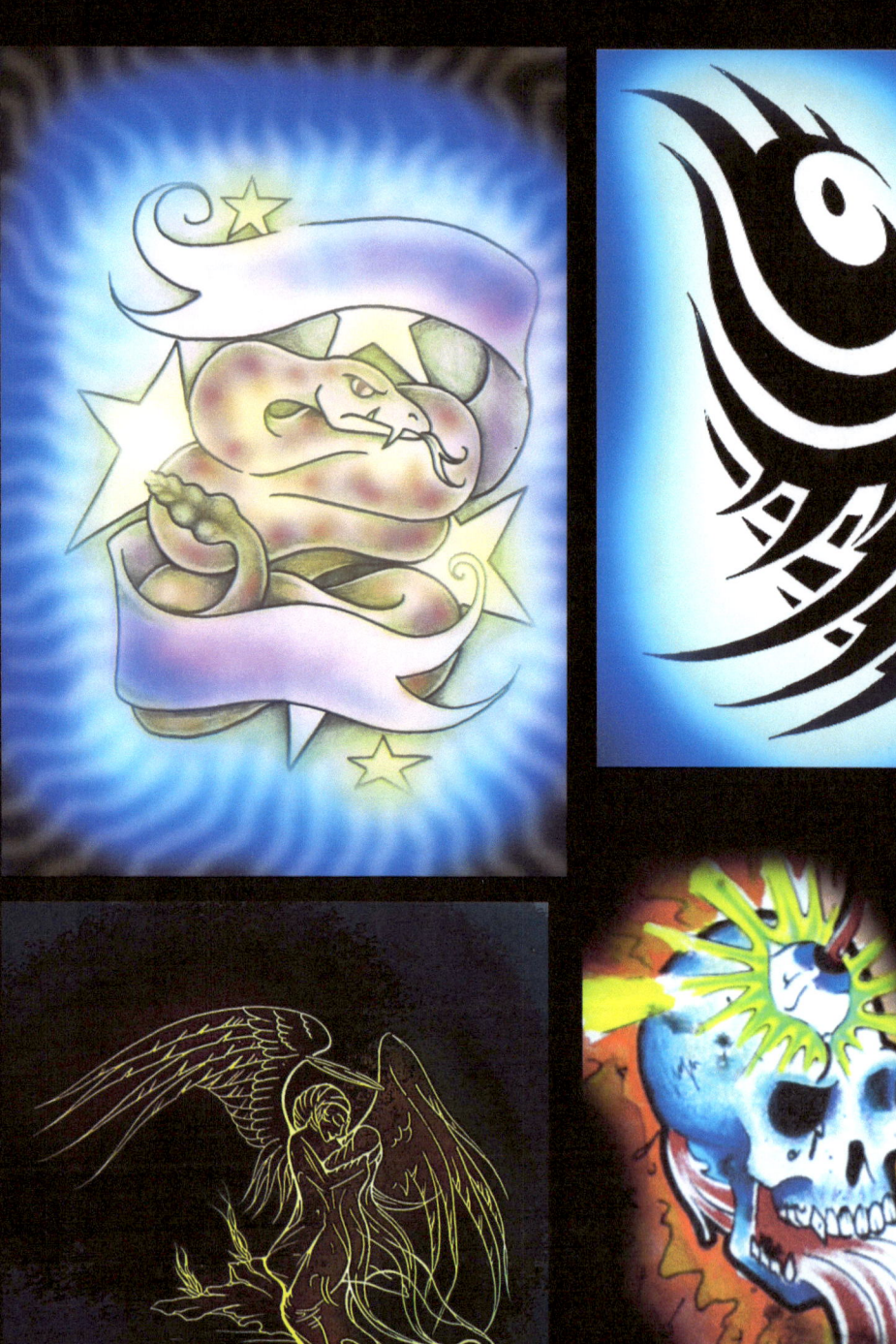

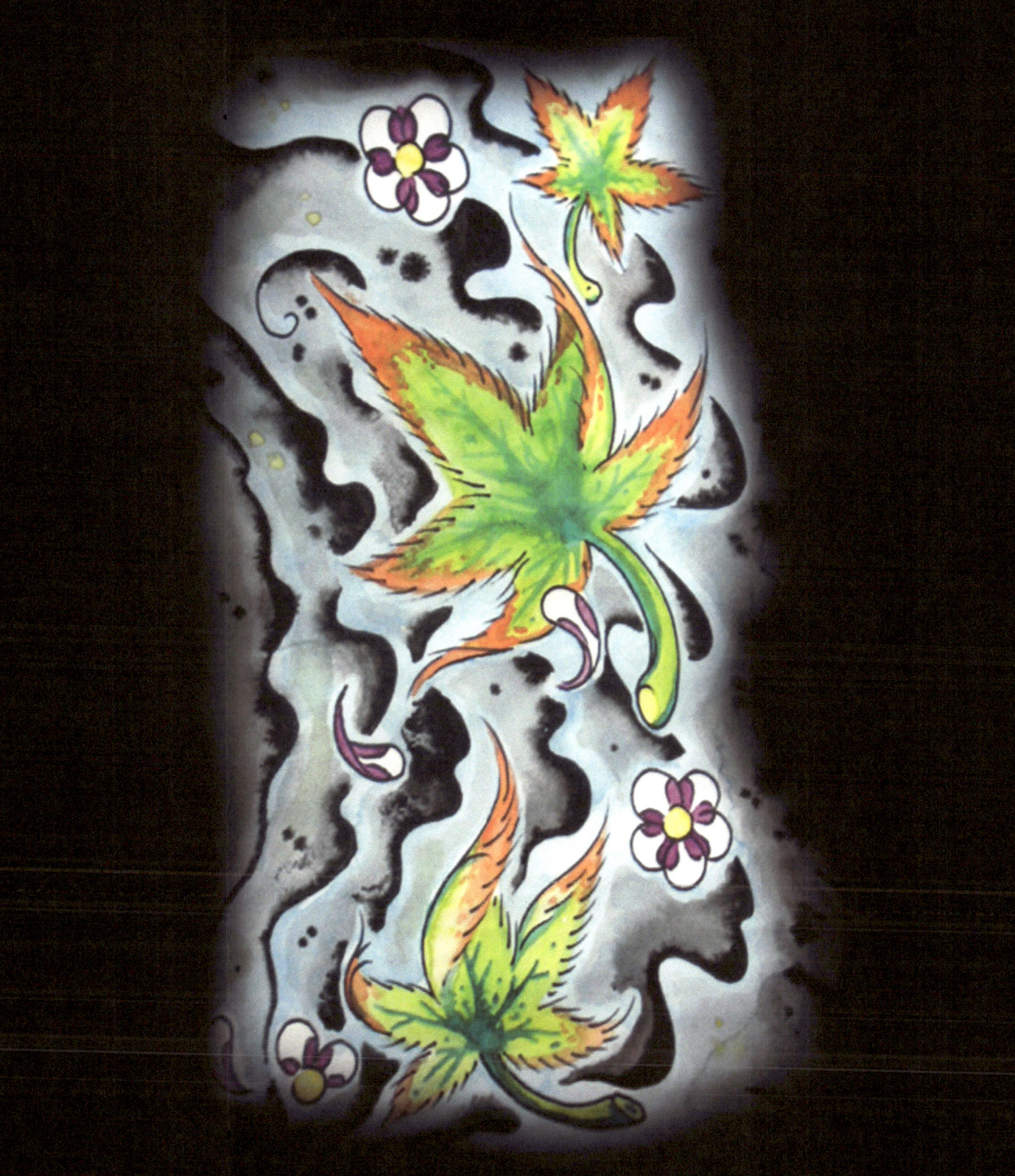

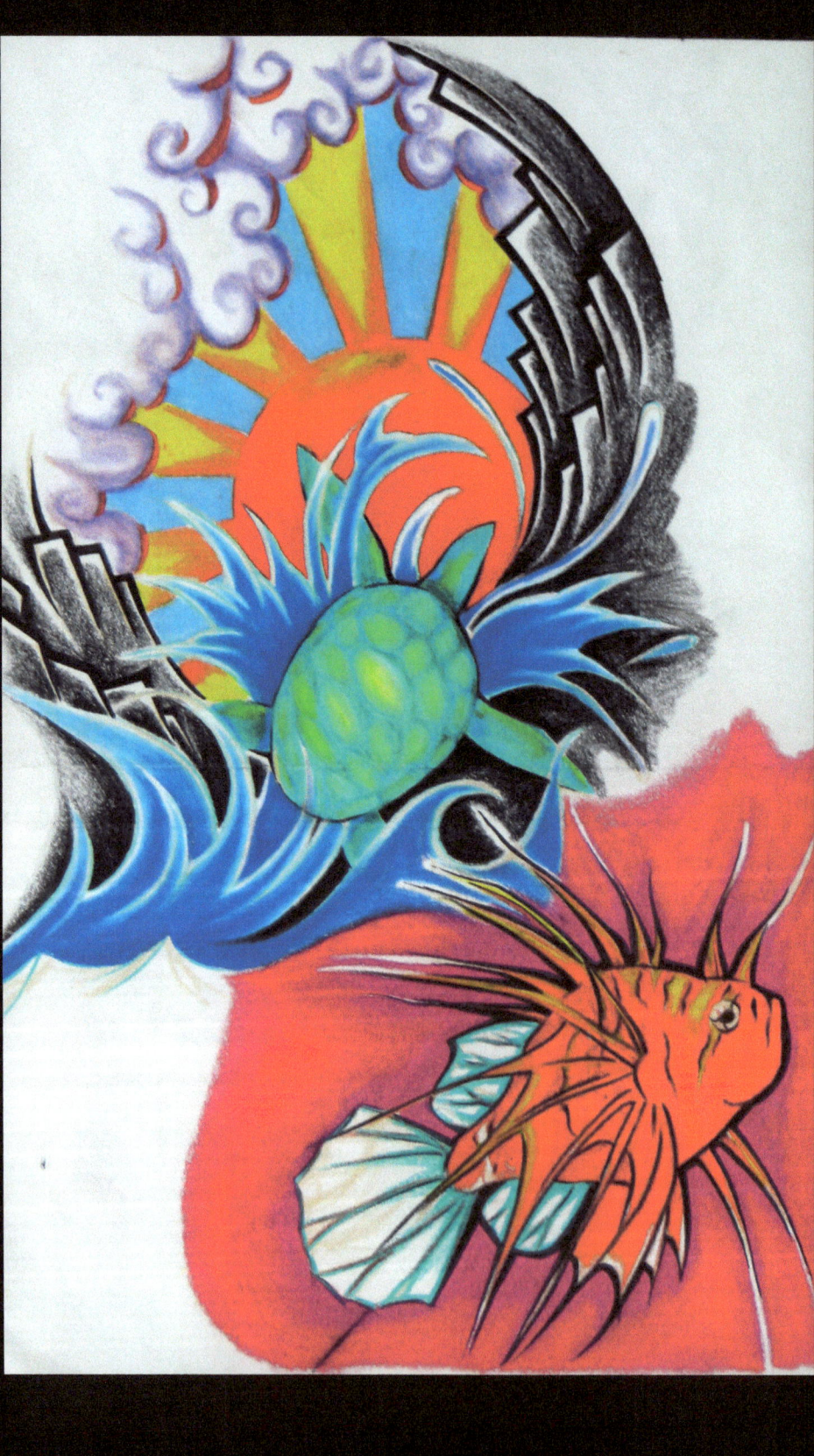

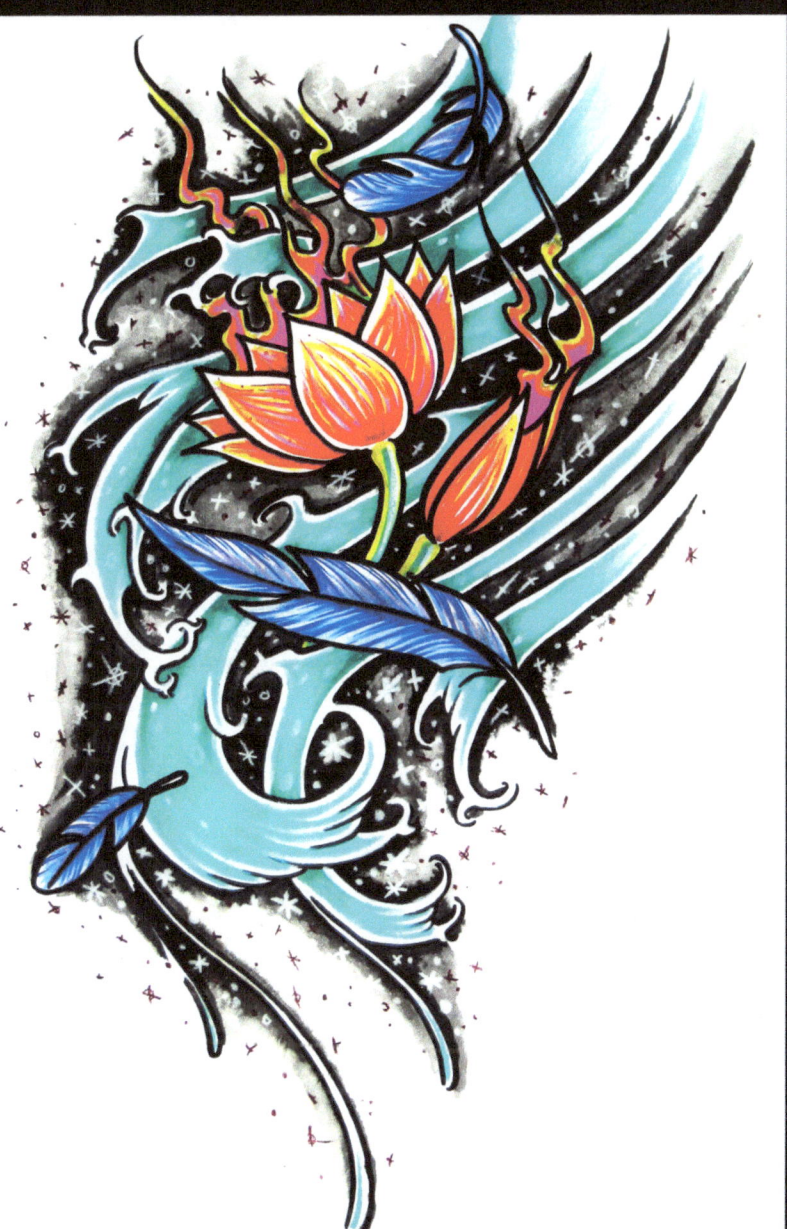

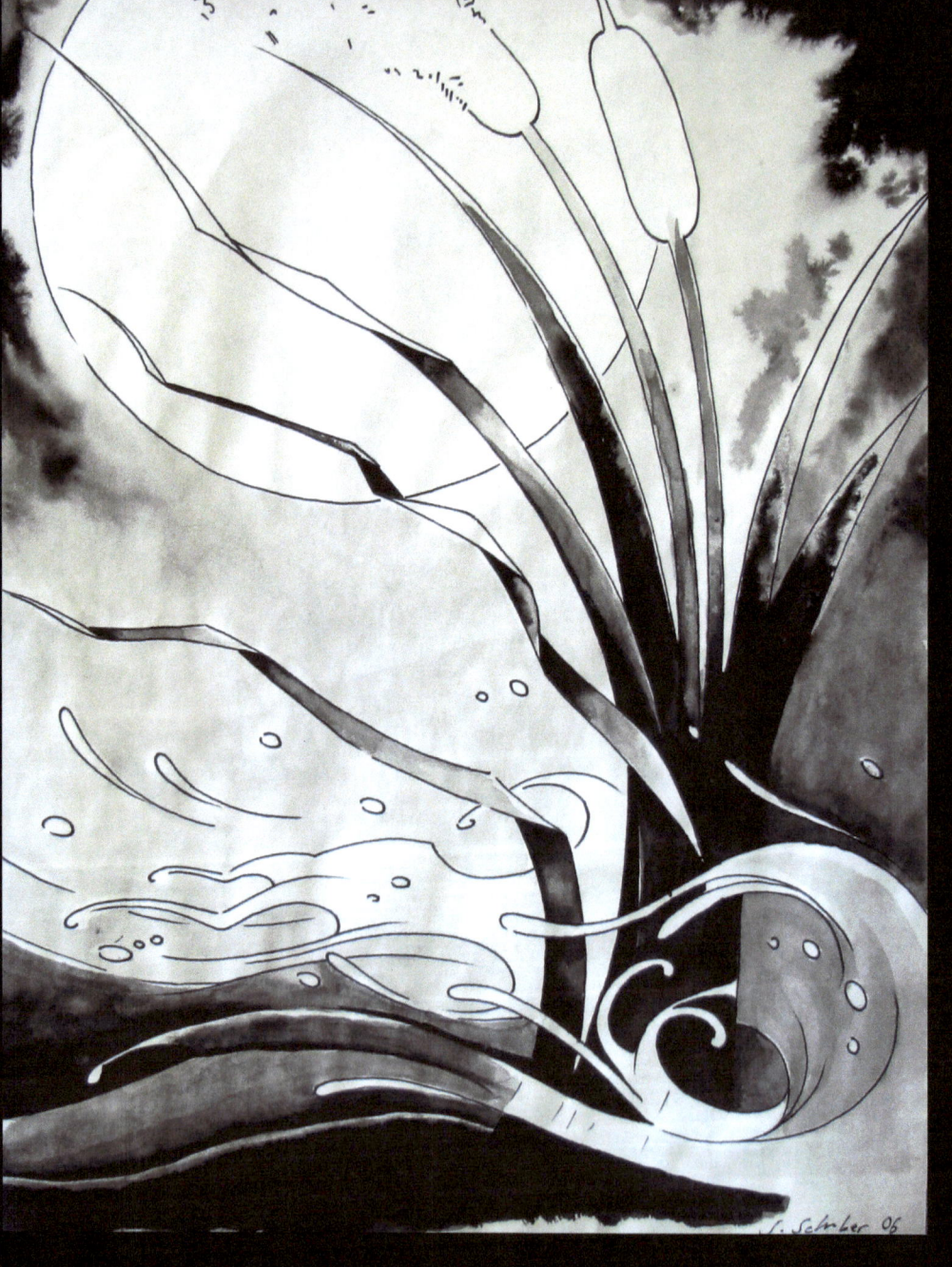

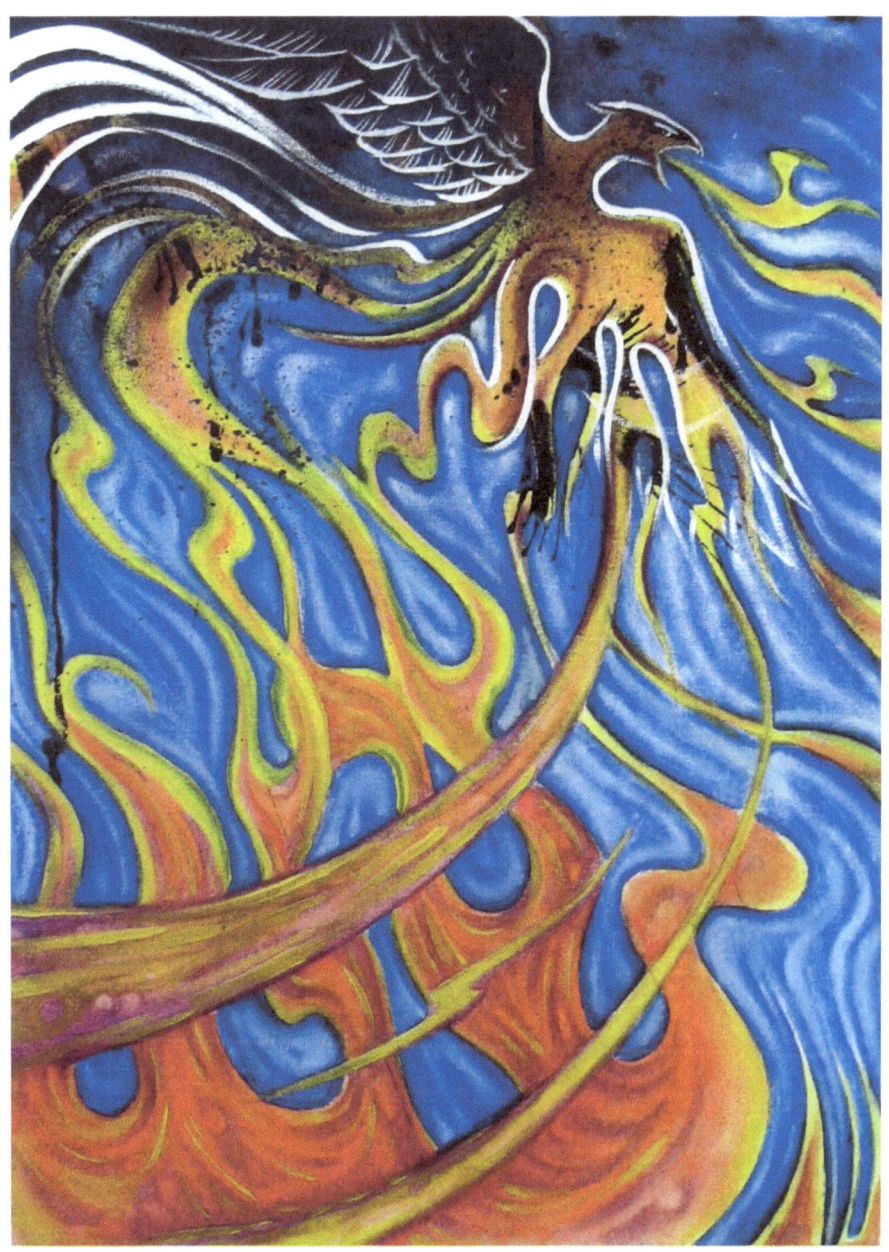

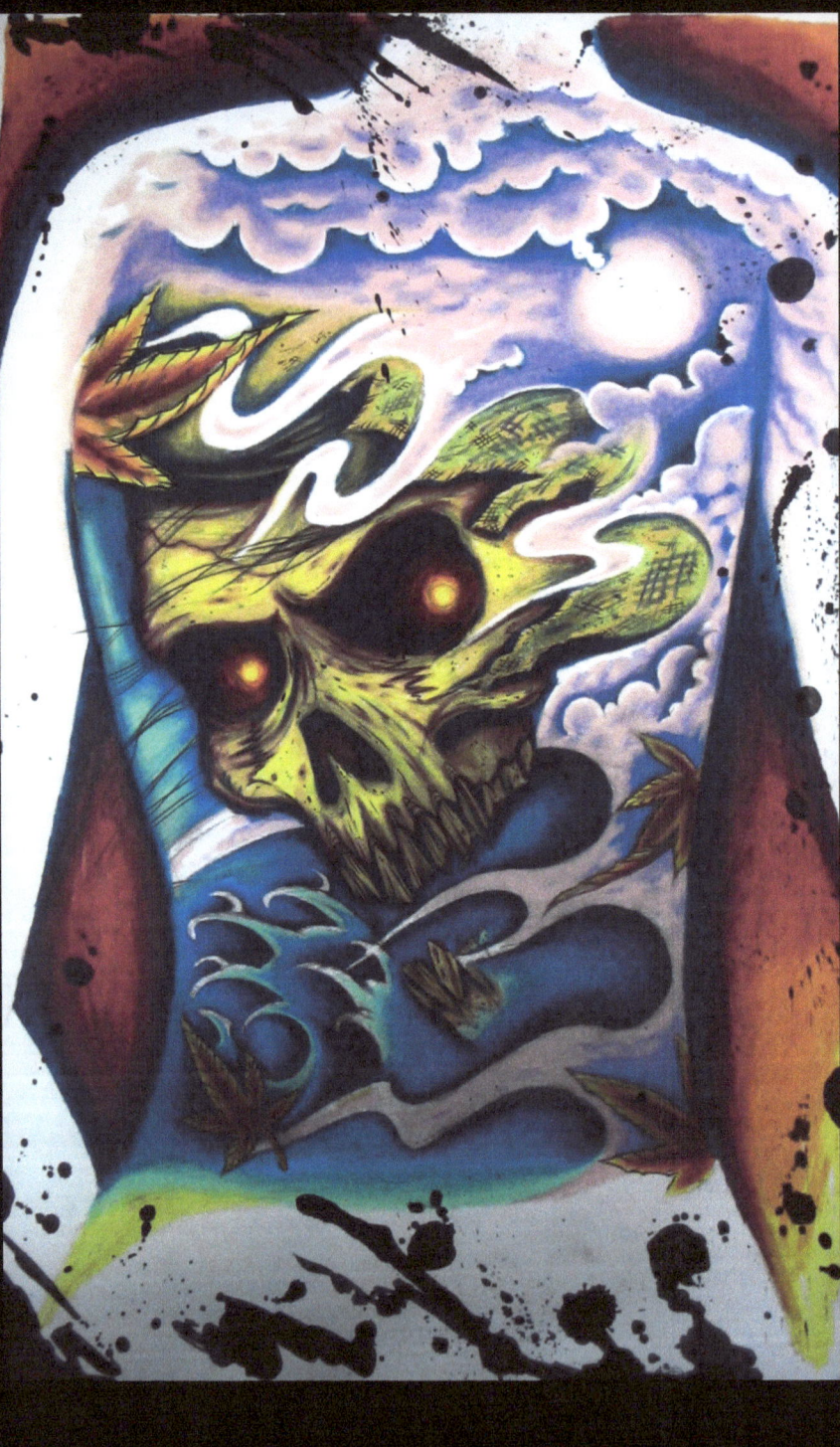

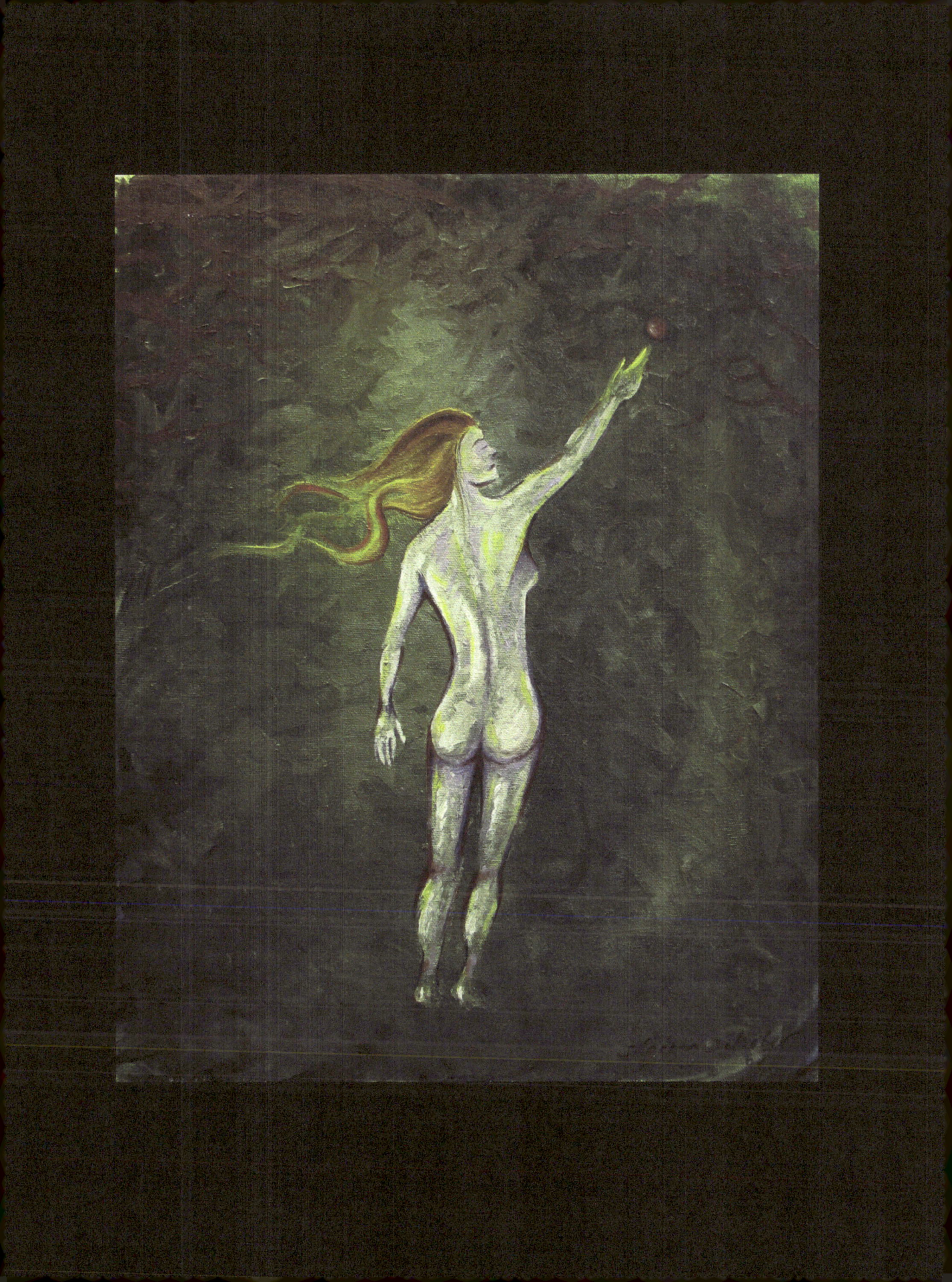

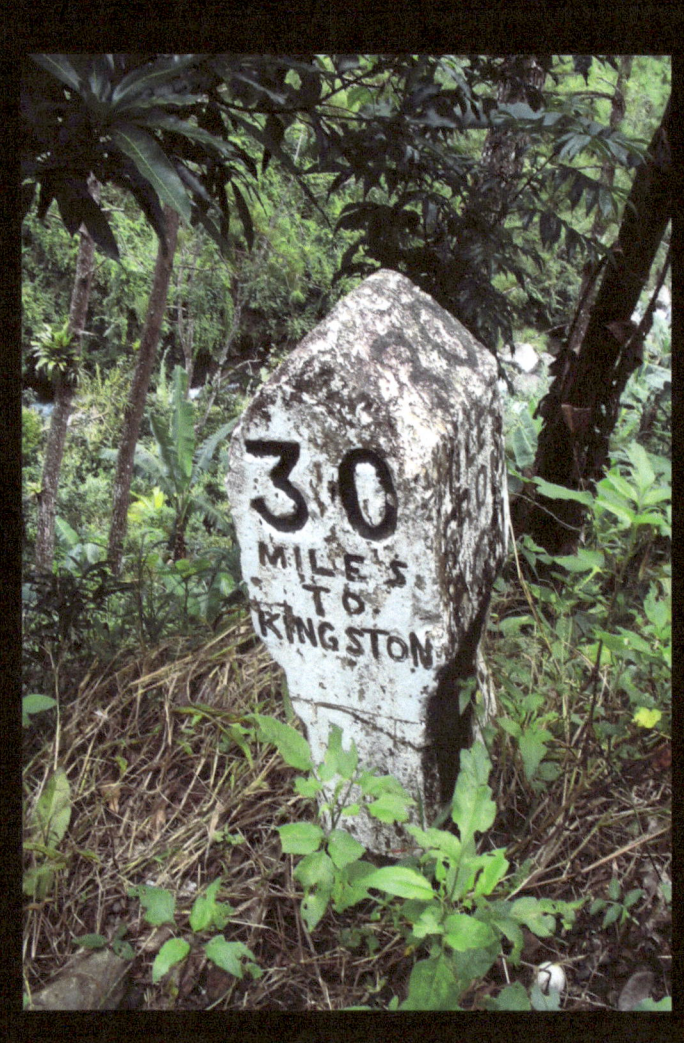